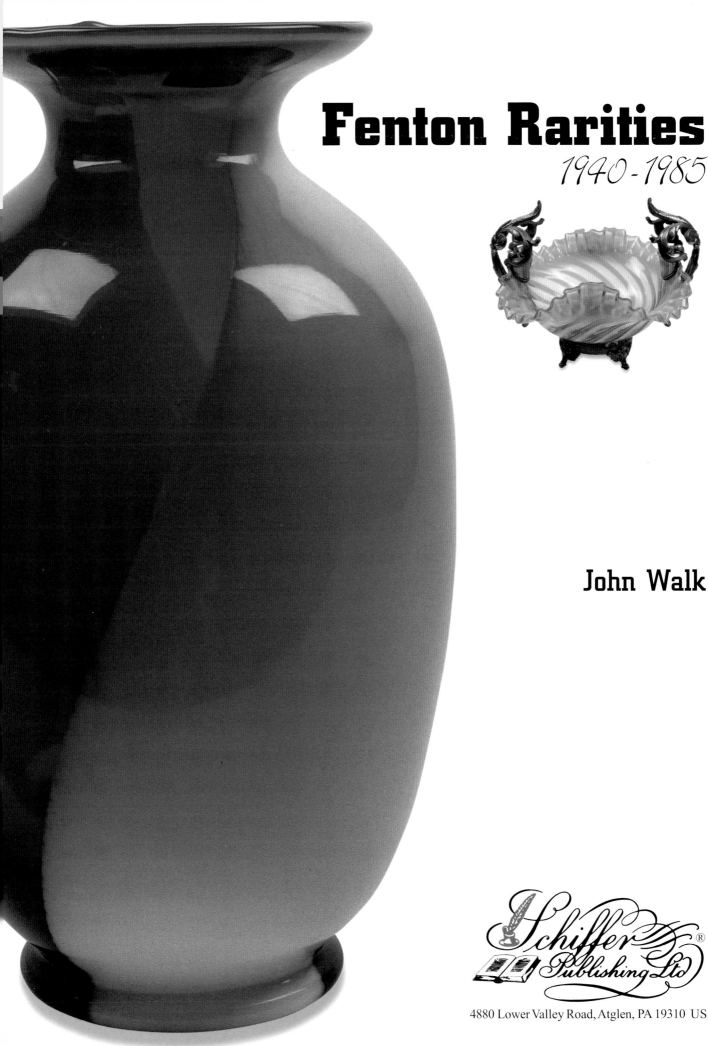

Fenton Rarities

1940-1985

John Walk

Schiffer Publishing Ltd

4880 Lower Valley Road, Atglen, PA 19310 USA

Dedication

To Linda and John Flippen, a couple who have contributed much to this book and who have inspired me to create this volume on Rarities and Whimsey items. Thanks so much for all the help, love, and support you have given me over the past few years. I don't know what I would do without the both of you!

Designed by Bonnie M. Hensley
Cover design by Bruce M. Waters
Type set in Zapf Chancery Mdlt BT/Aldine721 BT

ISBN: 0-7643-1595-1
Printed in China
1 2 3 4

Published by Schiffer Publishing Ltd.
4880 Lower Valley Road
Atglen, PA 19310
Phone: (610) 593-1777; Fax: (610) 593-2002
E-mail: Schifferbk@aol.com
Please visit our web site catalog at **www.schifferbooks.com**
We are always looking for people to write books on new and related subjects. If you have an idea for a book please contact us at the above address.

This book may be purchased from the publisher.
Include $3.95 for shipping.
Please try your bookstore first.
You may write for a free catalog.

In Europe, Schiffer books are distributed by
Bushwood Books
6 Marksbury Ave.
Kew Gardens
Surrey TW9 4JF England
Phone: 44 (0)20-8392-8585
Fax: 44 (0)20-8392-9876
E-mail: Bushwd@aol.com
Free postage in the UK. Europe: air mail at cost

Contents

Acknowledgments

My parents, John W. and Bonnie Walk, have my undying gratitude; if it wasn't for them, this book would not have been completed. So many times they have defended me over the duration of this project. They both were always there when I needed them, to fill in and to do bothersome chores while I was writing this book. They cared for me, listened to my fears and thoughts, and whole-heartedly supported me. Thank you from the bottom of my heart.

Over the past few years, my mother, who always has been close to me, accompanied me many times to take photos, in spite of her own health problems. She was a wonderful sounding board for setting pictures, gathering up glass around different houses, and even spotting items that I had missed in collections. Recently, I've come to wonder what I would do without her! I believe, because of this, we have become closer. I thank her for her sacrifices, help, and support.

I also want to thank Doris Frizzell, Dorothy Hines, Helen Fiaoni, and Jane Warner Smith; if it was not for these women, I would not be in business today, let alone doing this book. Over the course of the years, they have stood by me, have been my friends, inspired, and supported me in so many ways through their actions. I will always be indebted to them.

There is a couple, to which this book is dedicated, I came to know over the past ten years while doing the Nashville, Tennessee, Antique Market. From that time, I have grown to know and to love them dearly. They have taught me so much about glass in general. Linda and John Flippen are a special breed of collector, always ready to share their knowledge and advice on collecting. From John I gained insight on the making of glass, as he was a former employee of a plant that made auto glass. Although the product is different, the technique is the same! From Linda I have learn more than I ever hoped to on the histories of various types of Art Glass, including Fenton, especially in Cranberry Opalescent. She contributed much to this book, helping gather information, establishing what should and shouldn't be listed as rarities, and—as in previous books—watching prices at shows, shops, and Ebay. She talked to other collectors as well, all in an to attempt to determine the rises in prices and the demands for various item.

She has become a close personal friend, a sounding board on this and other books, and one that I can always depend on for anything. Linda and John Flippen are the kinds of friends that are seldom found. If it were not for their help, support, love, and encouragement, these books would never been completed.

Millie Cody is another person whose help, support, encouragement, and guidance I can never forget. Though I have not known her long, her friendship means more to me than anyone will ever know. She is another who, at any time, drops whatever she is doing and comes to assist in proofreading, typing, and many other jobs that went into this book. I can never thank her enough for being there.

Thomas K. Smith, of Indiana, has become a very close friend since I started work on the first book. He's always there to offer ideas and help with research and pricing. We have, over the past several years, traveled together a lot, doing both antique and glass shows, and I have come to admire his mind and his knowledge of all types of glass.

Audrey Elsinger has become a great sounding board on the value of items and has the insight to realize what item may be more scarce or rare than most believe. I thank her for her help on prices . . . determining what is rare, scarce, and not so scarce . . . and how rare is rare!

Jan Hollingsworth has been tremendously helpful in the 1970-1990 part of this book, as she had in past books, by giving me clues as to the idiosyncrasies of different items in many patterns. She has given me insight into which items were difficult to produce. Through many conversations, she has become a close friend and confidant.

So many other people have helped, have gave advice and support during the writing of this book. A few of these people are Dena & Allen Adden, Don Smith, Lee Garmon, Roserita Ziegler, Gail Ledbetter, Bonnie & Frank Zeller, and Alex James & Mike Robbins of James Antiques.

I want to extend a special thanks to Frank Fenton of the Fenton Art Glass Company and Fenton Glass Museum for his help, advice, and support. He seemed to think that I was crazy to even attempt such tasks as these books, but never tried to persuade me to drop them. Frank has done everything he could to help me. I am sure that the ordinary collector does not realize the dedication that he has for the glass that he and his family have produced for almost 100 years. He is always ready to answer questions, supply information, and help in any way that he can. He went over this and my other books several times, spending hours on them, checking facts, ware numbers, etc., to verify the information that I have put in them. I, like so many other people, would be lost without his knowledge and first-hand insights into when these items were made. I also want to thank Jennifer Maston, caretaker of the Fenton Glass Museum, who arranged for me to photograph the glass from the museum and was always ready to help whenever I needed a question answered or was looking for information.

Carolyn Kriner has also provided much for this book, not only furnishing glass, but also valuable information on different items. Over the years, she has contributed to many other books and projects on Fenton; but, I feel she has never received the proper acknowledgments that are due her. Her knowledge, on Fenton and L. G. Wright in the 1940-1970s time frame, is phenomenal. I owe her many thanks for making the time to have me in her home to take pictures and for taking time to go over slides and give me information on many of the items that were on them.

Another couple who allowed me to photograph their collection are Claire and Alan Kauffung, who opened the world of the Robert Barber art items, that Fenton produced in 1976, to me and who supplied valuable information on those items. Also, thanks to Dave Fetty, for adding to that information on many of the items that Dave himself produced while working with Robert Barber.

I feel the photographs are the main focus of a reference book on antiques. It is true, a picture is worth a thousand words. If it were not for these people, who opened their homes and collections, this book would of not of been possible. I am awed and humbled by their generos-

ity. The average person does not realize the efforts that these people go to in opening up their houses and lives to us, so we can come in to take pictures. Sometimes, because of the amount of glass, we are there for several days at a time. My thanks go out to all of you who kept us and welcomed us into your homes. Linda and John Flippen have not only became close friends, but have become family to us because of this. It seemed, if we were not taking pictures at their house, we would be staying there on the way to taking pictures elsewhere. Sharen and Al Creery are another couple who put up with us for a length of time and say they are anxious for us to come again; after the last time, I don't know whether they love us or are just crazy! Betty & Ike Hardman have had us in a total of three times in the past four years to take pictures. It is a wonder that you can keep digging through those rooms and still find items that you hadn't noticed before! Eileen and Dale Robinson deserve special thanks for having us, and putting up with us until past midnight. Audrey and Joe Elsinger also have my thanks for taking time out of a busy week to open their home to me.

Others who opened up their hearts, lives, and collections to us included:

The Fenton Glass Museum
Williamstown Antique Mall
Randy Clark Auctions
Linda & John Flippen
Lee Chadwell
Rich & Laurie Karman
Betty & Ike Hardman
Thomas K. Smith
Grody & Janice Bowerman
James Rose
Joe & Audrey Elsinger
Sharen & Al Creery
Jan Hollinsworth
Carol Toumlin
Susie & Ron Ballard
Mary Knight
Maxine Wilson
Andrew & Randi Jenkins
Wanell & Walt Jones
Connie & Steve Ducan of Kill Creek Antiques
Jan Hollingsworth
Alex James
Noralee and Ralph Rogers
Trudy and Dick Green
Chuck Bingham

Acknowledgments

Paula & Kevin Parker
Phyllis and Russell Heftly & Doris and Cletus McCallahan
    of Twins Antiques
Emogene Snyder
Dorothy Hines
Carolyn & Woody Kriner
Michael & Lori Palmer
Lynne & Gary Virden
Barbara Ryley
Vann Funderburk
Douglas Smith
LuAnn & Atlee Beene
Betty & Kenneth Hall
Darcie Smith
Carolyn & Dick Grable
Eva Fenton Kuhn
Sue Gomer
Claire & Alan Kauffung
William Lee
Phil Barber
Cindy and Rick Blais

Deb and Ed Volansky
Jackie Shirley
Millie Coty
Jesse & Bill Ramsey
Vickie Ticen
Doris Garjczyk

I want to extend thanks to the Fenton Art Glass Collectors of America and the Fenton Glass Society for the kindness, hospitality, encouragement, and support they showed me during the past few years at their conventions.

I also want to thank both the Fenton Finders Club of Kansas City for their help and hospitality during the Fenton Gala of 2000 and 2001, at which many of these pictures were taken.

Lastly, I want to thank Peter Schiffer of Schiffer Publishing for his support, encouragement, and help in this project. Also, thanks to the staff of Schiffer Publishing, including Jeff Snyder, my editor, who helped pull together this volume . . . and make sense of my ramblings!

Introduction

I know that, from the start, this book will have mixed reviews. I have been met with both reactions: "Why a book on rarities, as it almost impossible to find the common items?" and "When will it be out, I can hardly wait?" If you stop to think about it, the Fenton Art Glass Company, over the past sixty years, has produced many items that do not fall within the established categories of the regular product lines. Many such items are considered to be Fenton rarities and there are quite enough of them around to fill the pages of this book.

Furthermore, take into consideration that Fenton's is handmade glass. With that in mind, you look at the process of making this type of glass. Handmade glass itself gives the glass worker all the more opportunity to make a Whimsey, by creating a different ruffle than what was offered on the regular item or by adding a handle to a bowl or vase, thereby making a basket or creamer. With the workers were doing this on their own time, and also the higher ups, and designers at Fenton were forever trying something different in shapes, treatments, and colors for upcoming lines, it is possible for quite for a few pieces to be made as Whimsey or Sample items. Add to this the items for which, for one reason or another, a color, shape, or treatment just doesn't work and is quickly discontinued due to poor sales, public reaction, or problems in the design or production, and you end up with, over this time period, a lot of odd, offbeat, and unusual items. With this book, I hope not only to wet the collectors' interests in what is already known to be out there, but to make them aware that there might be more items that fall into this category—still undetected in attics, basements, and warehouses—than they might assume. Keep in mind that, at the time of this writing, all this glass is sixty years old, or less, and that a lot of original owners of it (or their children) are disposing of it due to old age and the dispersal of their homes. That being the case, there is a very good chance that many more items of this type will surface!

The Fenton Art Glass Company, especially during the 1940s, gave their workers the opportunity to make items on their own. Many of these items Frank Fenton refers to as having "walked out in their lunch box," which is how many of the Fenton whimseys have made it into the public domain.

Also keep in mind that at Fenton, when an item was made as a sample (also know as an experimental), it would sometimes be passed on to their sale associates in Chicago, Dallas, Kansas, etc., so they could test reaction to it in their area to see if it was sales worthy in either color, pattern, or shape. These samples were not returned to the factory and many times ended up being given away or disposed of in the areas to which they were sent. As for the rarities, they are just that, items that were in Fenton catalogs and, for some reason, did not last long. Sometimes such an item was even being discontinued before the catalog that it premiered in was out!

Several people asked me, in reference to the value of a book pertaining to this subject, if it would not be highly unlikely to own anything pictured in it. I told them to look at the Tucker Motor Club Association. This Club is devoted to the study and collection of Tucker Automobiles made in 1948. While there are less than fifty of these cars known to exist, there are several thousand members of this club. The majority of these members know that they will never own a Tucker Automobile! It is true, while a lot of these items are not one of a kind, it might be very uncommon for any more of them to surface. However, look at it this way, due to the increased interest of Fenton Art Glass, and the collecting of it over the past five years, there is more of a demand for accurate information on all aspects of this subject. Even if you don't find one single item that is pictured in this book, after reading and studying it, you will be more aware of certain shapes, colors, and patterns, increasing your chances of recognizing other items that Fenton made as whimseys or samples that you can add to your collection. My advice to the readers of this book is to study the beginning chapter, paying close attention to the Ware Number descriptions and familiarizing yourself with the shapes (and other basic shapes pictured in this book), as something else more spectacular or rare is sure to be lurking about!

The Difference Between a Rarity, A Sample Item, and a Whimsey

Before you begin to go through this book, it might be wise to realize the difference between a Rarity, a Sample (Experimental) item, and a Whimsey.

Rarity: An item, while in the regular Fenton catalogs, that was discontinued shortly after its introduction. It may have been discontinued due to problems in making the shape or color, due to the limited interest in it at the time of production, or even due to historically significant events (such as the shortage of uranium to produce Topaz Opalescent during World War II).

Sample Item: Made solely as an experimental item, to see if a certain color or treatment would work in a certain mould. Many times, Fenton would used moulds that were handy in the factory, but not in current production, to try out upcoming treatments and colors. This way they did not tie up production with moulds that were in regular use at the time. Keep in mind that both Fenton and other glass companies would not make just one item, in one color, during these Sample runs. They would produce at least a one-fourth turn to one-half turn, and some times a whole turn, depending on the complexity of the treatment and the item it was being made in (a "turn" is four hours of production, a "one-fourth turn" would be a single hour's production).

Whimsey: Made by a worker in his off time, at the factory, by changing a regular production item into an item of his own design, either by adding or leaving off a handle, changing a crimp, or even sometimes by gathering glass into a mould other than the color that it was meant to be in. These are the only items that can be truly classified as "one-of-a-kinds."

Pricing

The pricing of this book, because of its content and nature, was much more difficult than in my previous books. How can you determined prices for items that are seldom traded or offered for sale? In many cases, I will offer a very broad price range, reached by consulting dealers and collectors that are highly specialized and advanced. In many, many cases, however, UND will be listed, as particular items are too uncommon or unusual to attached a price too.

As always, it is up to the collectors themselves to decided what price is too high or too cheap. Many times I've seen people at shows I've sold at and attended pass up an item because they felt it was too high, an item a more experienced and knowledgeable collector leapt on eagerly because of its scarcity or uniqueness.

It is not the intention of this author to control or establish prices. As I am in the business of selling, I know that prices can sometimes be too high and that overpriced items will not sell.

Measurements

All measurements (and terms) are from factory catalogs or from actual measurements of the pieces. Actual measurements tend to vary widely from factory catalogs with handmade glass.

Special Note

Many people have asked me how to tell an item of Fenton Art Glass from an item made during the latter part of the nineteenth century, or from items that were made in Czechoslovakia in the 1920s and 1930s. Always keep in mind that, in most cases, the nineteenth century and Czechoslovakia blown items have the pontil mark in the base of the item. A Fenton item will not have a pontil mark; it will have a smooth bottom as it is blown from the top side, the top portion attached to the pontil was cut away, and the piece was then refired to form the ruffle. Some items from Czechoslovakia were made in this fashion also, but the ruffles are formed much sharper than Fenton's, and the glass itself doesn't have the look and feel of Fenton's.

History of the Fenton Art Glass Company

The Fenton Art Glass Company was organized in July 1905, in Martins Ferry, Ohio, by John, Charles, and Frank L. Fenton. It started as a decorating firm, buying other companies' glass blanks, decorating the items purchased, and then selling the painted glassware. As the Fentons became more competitive with their suppliers, it became necessary that the Fenton Art Glass Company manufacture their own glass.

In January 1907, the Fenton Art Glass Company opened its factory in Williamstown, West Virginia, on the site of the present factory. Their first factory manager was Jacob Rosenthal, creator of Chocolate Glass and Golden Agate. Rosenthal was formerly with the National Glass Company at its plant in Greentown, Indiana, the Indiana Tumbler and Goblet Co., and later with the Evansville Glass Company.

At the onset of manufacturing glass, the Fenton brothers entered the lucrative Carnival and Opalescent Glass market, landing large contracts with Butler Bros. and Woolworth's. Over the next twenty years, the Fenton Glass Company continued to prosper and grow.

In the early 1930s a decline began, which resulted in the most critical period of the company's history. Sales dropped to an all time low in 1933, causing the Fentons to consider closing their doors. Instead, the factory cut expenses, employees wages, and put off improvements in the factory. Money was borrowed from everywhere and insurance polices were mortgaged as orders fell off.

It was during the 1920s Fenton turned away from the now passé Carnival Glass, introducing a line of Stretch Glass and entering into the colored Depression Glass field in the early 1930s. Also added to the Fenton line was a grouping of Opaque colors that became quite popular, including Jade Green, Mongolian Green, Mandarin Red, Periwinkle Blue, Chinese Yellow, Ebony Black, and the now elusive colors of Flame and Lilac. A line of Satin Etch items was introduced in the mid-1930s as the Opaque colors waned in popularity.

It was in 1933 that Fenton introduced its line of mixing bowls and reamers for the Dormeyer company to sell with its electric egg beaters. It was that account that kept Fenton from folding during the depression years.

A cologne bottle, a copy of the old Hobnail pattern introduced in the late 1930s, pulled the Fenton Art Glass Company from the depths of the Depression and into economic renewal. It was in 1936 that L. G. Wright, a jobber based in New Martinsville, West Virginia (who used Fenton to make glass from moulds that he bought from defunct glass companies), brought in a mould of an old Hobb's Company barber bottle, hoping that Fenton would make a reproduction of it for his wholesale business. Through a chance of fate, a buyer for Wrisley Cologne saw the finished bottle and asked if it could be mass-produced. The original was too expensive to make, but it could be realigned to cut cost; so, the No. 289 bottle was born. The bottles were shipped to Wrisley, who filled and test marketed them in 1938. The result surprised both Fenton and Wrisley as the bottle sold better than they ever hoped, to the point that Fenton could not keep up with the demand. With the Wrisley and Dormeyer accounts, Fenton was quickly operating in the black again.

After seeing the success of the Hobnail cologne bottle, Fenton introduced a complete Hobnail line in 1939, which has become a company mainstay ever since; by far outlasting the Wrisley defection to a machine made bottle in the early 1940s.

Surprisingly, World War II brought a huge increase to Fenton's business in spite of labor and materials shortages. Some lines, such as Topaz Hobnail and Ivory Crest, were completely discontinued because of mineral shortages. Other lines were put on hold at different time until materials were once again available, and other lines were produced without certain chemicals and minerals, changing completely either the color or treatment of that glass (i.e. Blue Opalescent Hobnail became No Opalescent Blue Hobnail and Cranberry Opalescent Hobnail became Ruby Overlay Hobnail).

It was in the 1940s that "Abels Wasserburg" of New York started to buy Fenton products to decorate, as Fenton had done in its early days.

In 1948, the Fenton Company suffered a double loss when Frank L. Fenton passed away in May, followed by his brother Robert in November. This threw Wilmer C. and Frank M. Fenton, Frank L. Fenton's sons, instantly into the running of the company. Rumors spread quickly during this time that the company was in trouble and planned to fold, causing several major shareholders to sell their stock, which the younger Fenton brothers wisely and quickly bought in the wake of the turmoil.

In the early 1950s it was decided to abandon the independent jobbers, who were essentially in direct competition with the factory authorized stores. Though the cause of some hard feelings with some long time customers, this decision is one of the main reasons for Fenton's survival to this day.

At a time when handmade glass factories were closing rapidly, Fenton chose to expand to compete with the remaining old glass companies and to preserve the sales they had built up during the war. According to an expert in the glass business, the new owners were young and inexperienced and the stockholders lost faith. But, by breaking completely with the past, the Fenton company was able to push ahead. Business procedures were updated, new lines were developed, public relations were promoted, new equipment was bought, and new buildings were built. The product was also improved and strengthen until Fenton was proclaimed as the finest handmade glass in the U.S.

The late 1950s and early 1960s saw rapid rises in sales which surprised even the Fentons! During the mid-1960s, Fenton took advantage of its sales growth to expand its factory and offices. Many new personnel were added to expand the sales force and management of the company. The 1960s were banner years for Fenton.

In the late 1960s, Fenton again turned to hand decorating, with the able hands of Louise Piper and Tony Rosena, who quickly expanded that department into a profitable and long lasting venture. In 1970, Fenton announced the reintroduction of Carnival Glass, which had not been produced by Fenton since the 1920s. To ensure the value of the old pieces, Fenton embossed their name in the new pieces, a practice they would ultimately use on all their glassware. Adding to the strong sales of Carnival Glass in the 1970s was the reintroduction of Burmese, the development of Rosalene, the popular line of Satin Custard colors (along with Milk Glass in Hobnail and Silver Crest), and the still popular Cranberry Opalescent Hobnail.

In the late 1970s, the collector's appeal proved so popular that a collector's club was organized and is now going strong, holding annual conventions in Williamstown, West Virginia, ever summer. The Fenton Museum, dedicated to Fenton Glassware and all glass companies in the mid-Ohio valley, was opened on the second floor of the Fenton factory in 1977.

The 1970s again saw strong sales throughout the decade, in spite of rising cost of materials, union contracts, and expensive energy. In 1978, Frank Fenton decided to relinquish his position as president and became Chairman of the Board. He retired completely in 1985. Bill (Wilmer C.) became President in 1978 and then became Chairman of the Board in 1985 when Frank retired. In 1985, Bill relinquished the presidency to Frank's son, George W., but continued at Chairman of the Board. Frank continues as Vice President of Fenton Gift Shops, Inc. and Historian. Bill is still chairman of the board, President of the Fenton Gift Shop, and is actively involved in promoting the sale of Fenton glass on the QVC Home Shopping Network on cable TV. Their children now run the glass company.

The 1980s were the years of the Fenton company's greatest sales and also their biggest slump in sales. During that decade more glass factories closed and a poor economy developed. In 1979, sales were higher than ever; but, during the next several years a recession developed. Sales fell off and Fenton tried several new ventures in marketing to rebound. One of these, the QVC venture on television, has proven particularly successful. New marketing strategies and private mould work have also helped Fenton rebound from the slump of the 1980s and become stronger than ever.

Throughout the years, the Fenton Art Glass Company has survived tragedies, a devastating Depression, numerous recessions, and labor troubles to become the pre-eminent handmade glass factory that is not only known nation-wide, but world-wide.

Glossary

The Process Of Glass Making

A gather of glass is taken from the pot (furnace) of molten glass on the end of a long pipe and is handed to a person who is one of the blowers in the shop. After the piece is blown into the mould, it may then be given to the finisher who shapes it or crimps it. If a piece is a handled item, it is given to the handler who applies the handle. Finally, it is ready to take to the lehr to cool.

On blown ware, a gather of glass is taken from the melting furnace on the end of a long blowpipe and is handed to the blocker or blower. From the blower, who blows the glass into a mould, the piece may be sent to the annealing lehrs or sent to the finisher for further shaping. The piece may then be sent to the handler who adds the Basket handle. On pressed ware, the gather of glass is dropped into the mould; the presser cuts off the molten glass, and pulls the lever on the press, thereby lowering the plunger into the mould and forcing the glass into all parts of the mould. From there the piece may go to the finisher or handler or directly to the annealing lehrs for cooling.

Chemical List

Light Blue or Blue Opalescent	Copper oxide
Royal Blue	Cobalt oxide
Other Blues	Various combinations
of Copper, Cobalt, or	Chromium
Cranberry	Gold
Ruby	Selenium, Cadmium
and Sulfur	
Amethyst	Manganese oxide
Topaz	Uranium oxide
Emerald Green	Potassium Chromate
Black	Manganese, Cobalt and
Chromium	
Opal or Milk Glass	Fluorspar, Feldspar and
Sodium Silicofuroride	
Opalescent Glass	Fluorspar and Calcium
Phosphate	
Turquoise	Copper, Chromium,
Fluorine, and Aluminum	
Pink	Selenium and Neodymium

Terms and Phrases Used in the Glass Making Business

Batch: A mixture of sand, soda ash, lime, and other chemicals that modify the color or characteristics of the glass which is then inserted into the pot furnace or day tank that is heated to 2500 degrees Fahrenheit temperature, thereby resulting into the molted glass.

Blank: A blank is a piece of glass which has been formed and shaped and sent through the lehr and which is now ready to be processed by cutting, sand carving, or decorating, either by the company producing the blank, by a glass decorating company, or a glass cutting shop.

Blocker: The person who shapes the glass, fresh from the furnace, and blows the first bubble of air through a blow pipe into the glass.

Blower: The person who manipulates the glass into shape and plunges it into a mould. He then forces it throughout the mould by blowing into it.

Carrying-in Worker: The person who takes finished article to the Lehr for final cooling.

Carry Over Worker: The person who carries over pieces of glass, just pressed from the mould, to the glory hole for reheating so the finisher can put on a final crimp and shape in the glass.

D.C.: Term used for pieces that have a second, larger crimp besides the original smaller, tight ruffle on the pieces. (It might be noted that the first crimp is usually made by a crimping mould, while the second crimp is made by pulling the glass down by hand with a specific tool.)

Day Tanks: Direct fire furnaces in which glass is exposed to direct flames. Day tanks melt glass in twelve hours, which lets it be worked in the day time, and melts a new batch at night—or the other way around.

Finisher: The skilled worker who changes the shape of the piece, after it has come from the mould, into its final form, which may be flared, crimped, cupped, or changed into one of many different shapes.

Frit: Small pieces of crushed glass used in making Vasa Murrhina.

Gather: The still unformed glob of glass, fresh from the furnaces or day tank.

Gatherer: The worker who gathers glass from the day tank and takes it to the mould.

Glory Hole: A small furnace heated to a temperature to about 2500 degrees Fahrenheit which is used to reheat the glass so it can be reshaped by the finisher.

Hand Swinging: The process of reheating a tumbler or bowl or other item of glass to the point where it is so molten that it can be twirled on the end of the pipe like a baton so that centrifugal force will stretch the piece out into what we call a swung vase.

Handler: The worker who applies handles for baskets, jugs, etc.

Hot Metal Works: The area where furnaces are located in a glass factory.

Jobbers: Wholesalers who do not make the glass but who act as distributors for the glass company to the retail stores. The jobber may sell the regular Fenton, have glass made from the jobber's own moulds, or may have special glass made by the glass company from its moulds (sometimes in different colors or shapes) and then distributes it to the retailers throughout the jobber's territory.

Lehr: A long annealing oven heated to about 1000 degrees in which the glass is placed after it has been made in the Hot Metal Department. The glass is placed on a conveyor belt inside the oven. The stresses and strains that have been put into the glass during the process of heating and chilling are relieved by bring all the parts of the glass piece to the same temperature. Then the conveyor belt moves the glass to a cooler temperature and gradually cools it down to room temperature.

Mould Blown: Glass that is force blown into mould, either by mouth or air pressure.

NIL (Not in Line): Item was not sold in the regular line, of a certain treatment or color, nor was it offered in any of Fenton's catalogs, usually it was a Sample (experimental) item, to test the market, or an item that was produced, by special order, either for an individual, or another company, or jobber.

Off Hand Ware: Glass that is blown without moulds and shaped by the glass worker with hand tools.

Opaline Glass: Partially opaque glass that is translucent. It looks opaque but will transmit light. It is glass that is about halfway between transparent glass and opaque glass.

Opaque Glass: Glass that allows a limited amount of light to pass through it, showing little fire or translucence when held to light.

Overlay Glass: Cased glass in which one layer is gathered over another.

Pressed Blown: Glass pressed into the mould and then forced to fill out the mould by blowing into it, either by mouth or air pressure.

Presser: The skilled glassworker who controls the temperature of the mould, cuts off the glass when it is dropped by the gathers, controls the weight of the glass that goes into the mould, and pulls the lever of the press which brings the plunger down to force the glass into each part of the press mould. He removes the plunger and opens the mould to remove the glass.

Ringer: The worker who spins a thin ring of different colored molten glass to the edge of the piece, thereby forming the glass which we call Crest glass.

Spot mould: Sometimes called an optic mould. This mould is used to create an inner pattern in the glass. The mould itself has a pattern which is transferred to the glass. After reheating, the glass is then blown into a second plain mound with no pattern. When the piece is made from opalescent or other heat sensitive glass, by chilling and reheating, the patterns becomes opaque while other parts remain clear.

g-In Worker: The person who reheats the glass in the glory hole, removes it, and takes it to the finisher for further shaping.

Logos

The now famous "Fenton" in script, in an oval logo, was first used in 1970, only on Carnival Glass. Between 1972 and 1973, it was placed on Hobnail and other items. By 1975, almost all items made by Fenton had the logo.

In 1980, a small 8 was added to show the decade of the 1980s.

A small F in a logo was used in moulds that were acquired from McKee or moulds purchased from other glass companies. This practice was started in 1983.

The sand blasted logo was used on blown items or limited edition items, where other logos could not be seen. It was also used on off hand items and paste mould items. The sand blasted logo was used from 1980 to 1984.

The fancy script F logo was first sandblasted on Artisan and Connoisseur items beginning in 1984. It is used on items that do not have the regular logo impressed in the mould. Beginning in 1994, this fancy script F replaced the regular logo on all items that had not been previously marked. These items were primarily blown.

In 1990, a small 9 was added to the moulds to show the decade of the 1990s. In some cases, one has to look closely (as the numeral is so small) to determine that it is a 9 and not an 8.

Other markings include the 75th mark above the Fenton logo, used to designate the 75th anniversary items. This practice was continued for each anniversary issue thereafter.

The reader must keep in mind that, even though items made throughout the 1970s and after were to have been marked, there are many, many instances in which the logo was fired out or so faint it is easier to detect by rubbing it with your finger than by seeing it with the naked eye. The type of glass in which the logo was fired out was mostly cased blown ware, such as Cranberry. Sometimes the logo is so faint on these items that all you can make out is part of the oval!

Chapter One
Ware Number Description

In July 1952, Fenton began to assign individual ware numbers to each item. After that time, the ware number included four numerals and two letters. The letters showed the color or decoration, and the numerals showed the pattern and shape. Before July 1952, the mould numbers showed pattern or mould shape and needed a word description following the number to describe decoration and color. Example: All Hobnail pieces have the same number, 389; all melon shaped pieces were 192. All sizes and shapes from the same shaped or patterned mould carried the same number. In the pictures to follow are the major moulds that Fenton used from 1940 to 1952 and the ware numbers assigned to them. In the pictures following that are many of the major shapes that were in use from 1952 to 1985, listed with most of the patterns that they were

made in. We did not attempt to picture embossed patterns, made during this time period, such as Water lily, Hobnail, Roses, and many others that were produced during the 1970s in Carnival, Satin, and other treatments as we feel the readers have become aware of these items, by pattern alone; however, we are picturing basic moulds to make the reader more aware of their shapes, and also items, treatments, and patterns that were made off of them so the reader might recognize, from shape alone, a sample item or whimsey. Although there are other moulds that were periodically used, these were the shapes that were in use most regularly. In the cases when a mould had been used prior to the issue of its Ware Number, it will be listed under the mould number and, at the end of that description, it will note the Ware Numbers that were used from that mould.

#36: Footed Vases 4" Fan Vase, 4" D.C. Vase, 6" Fan Vase, 6" D.C. Vase. Made in Aqua Crest, Emerald Crest, Gold Crest, Rose Crest. After 1953 in the Crest Line these were referred to as: #7375 6.25" Fan Vase; #7355 4.5" Fan Vase; #7356 6.25" DC Vase; #7354 4.5" DC Vase. The items in Chapter One are displayed solely to aid the reader in shape identification. Values for the items in this chapter may be found in my previous volumes: *The Big Book of Fenton Glass, 1940-70; Fenton Glass Compendium, 1940-70;* and *Fenton Glass Compendium, 1970-85.*

#37: Mini Baskets, Mini Fan Vases, Mini Vases. Made in Aqua Crest, Gold Crest, Blue Opalescent, French Opalescent, Topaz Opalescent.

#38: Mini Hand Vase. Made in Blue Opalescent, French Opalescent, Topaz Opalescent.

#91: Candy Dish (Candy Dish on Right Side of Picture). Made in Blue Opalescent Coin Dot, French Opalescent Coin Dot, Cranberry Opalescent Coin Dot.

#71: (later #9020) Shell-shaped Bowl. Made in Blue Satin 1952; Peach Satin and Green Satin 1952-54; Lilac 1955; Peach Crest 1955-64.

#92: Dresser Set. Made in Blue Opalescent Coin Dot, French Opalescent Coin Dot, Cranberry Opalescent Coin Dot.

#93: Candy Dish. Made in Blue Opalescent Coin Dot, French Opalescent Coin Dot, Cranberry Coin Dot. Also known in Ivy Overlay.

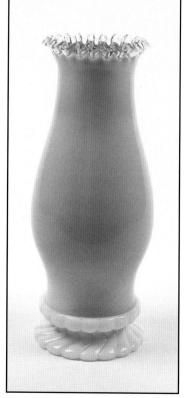

#170: Hurricane Lamp/Base. Made in Peach Crest, Ruby, Amber, Green Snow Crest, Mulberry Overlay, Ruby Overlay (Diamond Optic).

#184: Vase. Made in 6"/8"/10"/12" sizes. Made in Aqua Crest, Gold Crest, Peach Crest, and Opalescent Dot Optic.

#183: 10" Vase. Made in Ivory Crest, Blue Ridge, All Opalescent Swirl Colors.

#186: 8" Vase. Made in Aqua Crest, Gold Crest, Peach Crest, Rose Crest, Silver Jamestown, Blue Overlay, Rose Overlay, Ivy Overlay, All Opalescent Swirl Colors, and Blue Ridge, in the Barcelona Pattern. Later known as #7258 8" Vase and #7250 8" Vase (Jack in Pulpit Crimp).

#187: 7" Vase. Made in Peach Crest, Aqua Crest, Gold Crest?, Rose Crest?

#189: 10" Vase. Made in Blue Opalescent Coin Dot, Cranberry Opalescent Coin Dot, French Opalescent Coin Dot, Aqua Crest, Gold Crest?, Rose Crest?

#192: Melon Line. Made in 10" Basket, 10" Bowl, 3 sizes of Colognes, Squat Candlestick, 5.5" Jug, 6" Jug, 8" Jug, Squat Jug, Candy/Large Powder Jar, 5"/5.5"/6"/8" Vases. Made in Peach Crest, Blue & Rose Overlay, Mulberry Overlay, Ruby Overlay. Some pieces are also known in Aqua Crest, Gold Crest, and Rose Crest.

#192A: Melon Line Variation. Made in 9" Jug, 9" Vase, Small Powder Jar, and Small Cologne. Made in Peach Crest, Blue & Rose Overlay, Mulberry Overlay, Ruby Overlay, also some pieces known in Aqua Crest, Gold Crest, and Rose Crest.

#193: 11" Hand Vase. Made in Peach Crest, also known in Aqua Crest, Azure Blue, Gold Crest, Ruby Overlay, and Mulberry Overlay. Later known as #5155 11" Vase.

#194: Vases 6"/8"/11"/13". Made in Blue Opalescent Coin Dot, Cranberry Opalescent Coin Dot, French Opalescent Coin Dot, Honeysuckle Coin Dot (except 13" size); in versions of 1 Handle, 2 Handles, no Handles. Also made in 6", 8", and 11" sizes in Ivy Overlay and the 8" size in all colors of Snow Crest. Later known as the #1452 11" Vase; #1459 8" Vase; and #1472 6" Vase.

#201: 5" Vase. Squat Jug; Made in Blue Opalescent Coin Dot, Cranberry Coin Dot, French Opalescent Coin Dot, Honeysuckle Coin Dot, Lime Green Coin Dot. Made in 5" Vase in Aqua Crest, Gold Crest, Ivory Crest, Peach Crest, all colors of Snow Crest, all colors of Spiral Optic, Blue Ridge, and Rose a& Blue Overlay. Made in 5" Rose Bowl in Blue Ridge, Spiral Optic in French Opalescent, Green Opalescent, Blue Opalescent, Cranberry Opalescent, Polka Dot in Cranberry Opalescent, and in Peach Blow.

#203: 7" Basket, 7" Bowl, 4" Rose Bowl, 4.5" Vase. Made in Blue Opalescent Coin Dot, Cranberry Coin Dot, French Opalescent Coin Dot, Honeysuckle Coin Dot, Lime Green Coin Dot, Aqua Crest, Emerald Crest, Gold Crest, Ivory Crest, Peach Crest, Rose Crest, all colors of Snow Crest, Blue & Rose Overlay, Ruby Overlay, and Mulberry Overlay. Also know in a "Special" Basket in Aqua Crest, Gold Crest, Ivory Crest, Peach Crest, and Rose Crest. Later known as #7227 7" Bowl; #7237 7" Basket; #7254 4.5" Vase.

#208: Handled Cruet, 5" Vase. Made in Blue Opalescent Coin Dot, Cranberry Coin Dot, and French Opalescent Coin Dot.

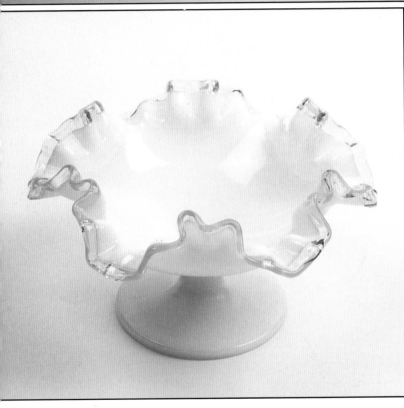

#206: Footed Comport. Made in Aqua Crest, Emerald Crest, Gold Crest, and Rose Crest. Also done in Blue Pastel, Rose Pastel, Turquoise Pastel, and Green Pastel Milk Glass. Later known as the #7228 Footed Comport.

#389: Hobnail Line. Consists of Baskets, Bonbons, Bowls, Colognes, Candy Dishes, Colognes, Powder Dishes, Jugs, Vases, Etc. Made originally in Blue Opalescent, Cranberry Opalescent, French Opalescent, Green Opalescent, and Topaz Opalescent.

17

#401: Flower Pot. Made in Emerald Crest and Emerald Snow Crest.

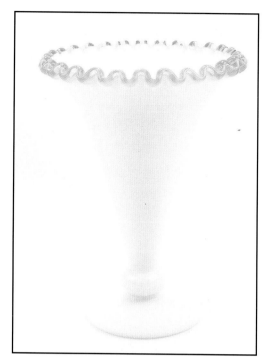

#573: 8" Vase. Made in Fan and D.C. Shape. Made in Aqua Crest, Gold Crest, and Rose Crest.

#510: 8" Vase. Made in Fern Optic, Rib Optic, & Diamond Optic Satin Opalescent.

#680: Crest Pattern. Made in Plates, Cups, Saucers, Bowls, Oil Bottle, Creamer, Sugar, Mayo, Nut Dish, Etc. Made in Aqua Crest and Emerald Crest. Cups known to exist in Rose Crest.

#680: Crest Pattern. Made in Plates, Cups, Saucers, Bowls, Oil Bottle, Creamer, Sugar, Mayo, Nut Dish, Etc. Made in Aqua Crest and Emerald Crest.

#682: 10" Low Bowl, 12" Plate. Made in Aqua Crest, Gold Crest, Ivory Crest. Jade with Milk Crest and Jade Crest.

#705: Footed Ivy Ball. Made in Green/White Foot, Ruby Overlay/White Foot, Amethyst/White Foot, Jamestown Blue/White Foot, Polka Dot in Cranberry with Crystal Foot.

#711: Beaded Melon Line. Made in 7" Basket, 10" Basket, 4"/5" Rose Bowl, 7" Bowl, 10" Bowl, 2 sizes of Colognes, Creamer, Candy, Powder Dish, 5.5"/6"/8"/9" Jugs, Squat Jug, Tumbler, Mini Bud Vase, and 4"/5"/5.5"/6"/8"/9" Vases. Made in Peach Crest, Blue Overlay, Green Overlay, Amber Overlay, Yellow Overlay, and Ivy Overlay. Also known in Aqua Crest in 7" Basket and Emerald Crest. Not in all colors in all shapes.

19

#815: Cruet. Made in Fern Optic, Rib Optic, Diamond Lattice Optic, and Swirled Feather in Blue Satin, Rose Satin, and French Satin.

#814: Large Bottle/Stopper. Made in Blue Opalescent Coin Dot, Cranberry Coin Dot, and French Opalescent Coin Dot.

#894: Decanter, 10" Vase. Both made in Blue Opalescent Coin Dot, Cranberry Coin Dot, French Opalescent Coin Dot, 10" Vase only in French Opalescent, Blue Opalescent, Cranberry Opalescent Spiral Optic, Blue Ridge, Ivory Crest, and Peach Crest Decanter. Also made in Ruby Overlay, Mulberry Overlay, and Cranberry Spiral Optic.

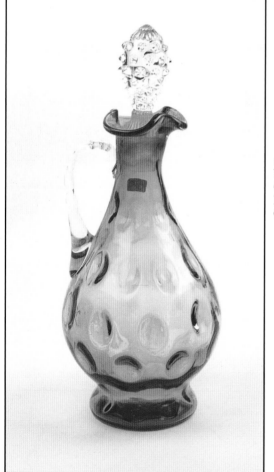

#951: Cornucopia Candlesticks. Made in Aqua Crest, Gold Crest, Ivory Crest, and Rose Crest.

#1353: Handled Jug, 10" Vase, Tumbler. Jug and Tumbler made in Coin Dot Opalescent colors of: Blue Opalescent; French Opalescent, Honeysuckle, and Cranberry. Peach Crest, Ruby Overlay, and Mulberry Overlay. Vase made in Coin Dot Opalescent colors of: Blue Opalescent, French Opalescent, Honeysuckle and Cranberry. Aqua Crest, Gold Crest, Ivory Crest, Peach Crest, Rose Crest, Mulberry Overlay, and Ruby Overlay. Tumbler made in Mulberry Overlay and Ruby Overlay.

#1522: 10" Bowl, 10" Basket, Covered Candy. Made in Blue Opalescent Coin Dot, Cranberry Opalescent Coin Dot, French Opalescent Coin Dot, Aqua Crest, Gold Crest, Ivory Crest, Peach Crest, Rose Crest, and Spiral Optic (all colors). Bowl also made in Snow Crest. Candy only in Coin Dot and Spiral Optic colors.

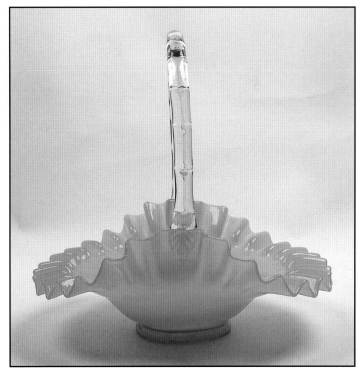

#1524: Candlestick. Made in Blue Opalescent Coin Dot, Cranberry Opalescent Coin Dot, and French Opalescent Coin Dot.

#1523: 13" Bowl, 13" Basket, Hollow Candlesticks. Made in Aqua Crest, Gold Crest, Ivory Crest, Peach Crest, and Rose Crest.

21

#1720: 7.5" Pinch Vase. Made in Fern Optic, Diamond Optic, Rib Optic, and in Satin Opalescent colors. Also in Ruby Overlay, Green, Ruby, and Amber Snow Crest. Honeycomb Optic in Green and Blue Overlay. Later known as the #2451 7" Pinch Vase.

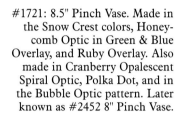

#1721: 8.5" Pinch Vase. Made in the Snow Crest colors, Honeycomb Optic in Green & Blue Overlay, and Ruby Overlay. Also made in Cranberry Opalescent Spiral Optic, Polka Dot, and in the Bubble Optic pattern. Later known as #2452 8" Pinch Vase.

#1920: 12" Top Hat (largest hat in picture). Made in Peach Crest, Blue Ridge, and Spiral Optic in all colors.

LEFT: #1921: 10" Top Hat, 10" Vase. Made in Peach Crest, Blue Ridge, and Spiral Optic in all colors. 10" Top Hat only in Snow Crest Colors. The 11" Basket was made in Spiral Optic colors, Peach Blow, Peach Crest, Ivory Crest, and Blue Ridge. RIGHT: #1922: 8" Top Hat, 10" Basket, 9" Vase. Made in Peach Crest, Peach Blow, Ivory Crest, Aqua Crest, Blue Ridge, and Spiral Optic in all colors.

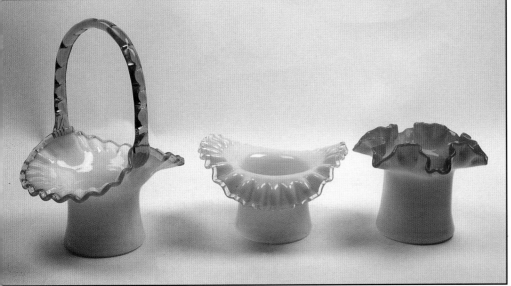

#1923: 7" Top Hat, 7" Basket, 7" Vase. Made in Aqua Crest, Gold Crest, Ivory Crest, Peach Crest, Blue Ridge, and Spiral Optic in all colors. Top Hat also in Snow Crest.

#1924: 5" Top Hat, 5" Basket, 5" Vase, Tall Creamer, Creamer & Sugar. Made in Blue Opalescent Coin Dot, Cranberry Coin Dot, French Opalescent Coin Dot, Aqua Crest, Gold Crest, Ivory Crest, Peach Crest, Rose Crest, Blue Ridge, Spiral Optic in all colors, Rose & Blue Overlay, Green Overlay, Amber Overlay, Yellow Overlay, Ivy Overlay, Mulberry Overlay, and Ruby Overlay. Top Hat made in Snow Crest. Tall Creamer, Sugar & Creamer made in Blue Opalescent Coin Dot, Cranberry Coin Dot, and French Opalescent Coin Dot. Tall Creamer made in Peach Crest, Blue Ridge, Spiral Optic, Blue & Rose Overlay, Mulberry Overlay, and Ruby Overlay.

#1925: 6" Vase, 8" Vase, 6" Basket. Made in Blue Opalescent Coin Dot, Cranberry Coin Dot, French Opalescent Coin Dot, Aqua Crest, Peach Crest, Snow Crest, Rose & Blue Overlay, Ivy Overlay, and in 5" size in the Snow Crest colors. Later known as the #7256 6" Vase.

#1934: 6" Vase, Handled Jug. Made in Blue Opalescent Coin Dot, Cranberry Opalescent Coin Dot, and French Opalescent Coin Dot. Jug made in Rose and Blue Overlay.

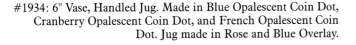

23

#3001/3003: 6" Vase, 8" Vase. Made in Blue Overlay, Cranberry Spiral, Yellow Overlay, and Ivy Overlay.

#3004: 8.5" Vase. Made in Snow Crest colors.

#3005: 11" Vase in Cranberry Coindot and the Snow Crest colors. Later known as the #7251 11" Vase.

#4516: 9" Vase. Made in Snow Crest colors, also in Blue and Rose Overlay.

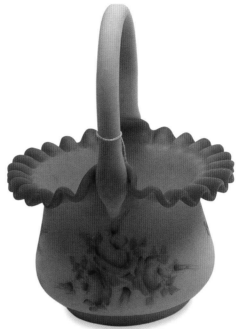

#1637: 7" Deep Basket. Made in Plated Amberina and Opaque Blue, Colonial Blue, Amber, and Orange in the Diamond Optic pattern, (Mould #1737), and Burmese with Decorated Roses (Mould #7238).

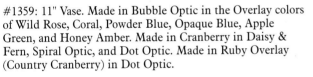

#1359: 11" Vase. Made in Bubble Optic in the Overlay colors of Wild Rose, Coral, Powder Blue, Opaque Blue, Apple Green, and Honey Amber. Made in Cranberry in Daisy & Fern, Spiral Optic, and Dot Optic. Made in Ruby Overlay (Country Cranberry) in Dot Optic.

#1680: Covered Candy. Made in Plated Amberina and Opaque Blue, Colonial Blue, Amber, and Orange in the Diamond Optic pattern, (Mould #1780), Spiral Optic, in Blue Opalescent and Cameo Opalescent (Mould #3180), and Burmese, with Decorated Roses (Mould #7284).

#5858: 8" Wheat Vase. Made in the 1960s Overlay colors of Wild Rose, Coral, Powder Blue, Opaque Blue, Apple Green, & Honey Amber; Milk Glass, Silver Crest; Country Cranberry; 1980s Overlay colors of Dusty Rose, Federal Blue, Heritage Green, Periwinkle Blue; & Candleglow Yellow; and in the decorated Opal pattern of Petite Fleur.

#6459: 11" Melon Vase. Made in all Vasa Murrhina colors. The Overlay colors of Dusty Rose, Federal Blue, Heritage Green, Periwinkle Blue, & Candleglow Yellow, Country Cranberry, Rose Satin, Silver Crest, Violets in The Snow, and Satin Decorated Patterns of Daisies on Custard & Pink Blossoms.

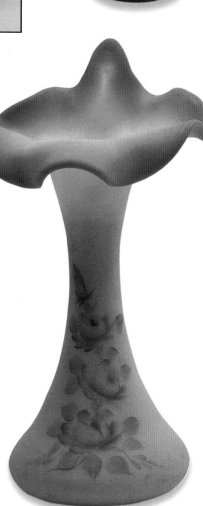

#7252: 7" Vase. Made in 1960s Overlay colors of Wild Rose, Coral, Powder Blue, Opaque Blue, Apple Green, & Honey Amber (Mould #1356); Silver Crest; Violets in the Snow; Cardinals in Winter; Decorated Butterflies; Rose Satin; Custard Decorated patterns of Blue Dogwood; Blue Roses on Blue Custard; Chocolate Roses; Clydesdales; Daisies on Custard; Daisies on Cameo; Log Cabin; Pink Blossoms; Burmese patterns of Roses on Burmese; Autumn Leaves on Burmese and Scene on Burmese.

#7255: 11" Tulip Vase. Made in Decorated Satin patterns of Blue Roses on Blue Satin, Daisies on Cameo, Sunset, Burmese patterns of Roses on Burmese, and Pink Dogwoods on Burmese.

#7254: 4" Vase. Made in Peach Crest, Apple Blossom, Violets in the Snow, Butterflies on Silver Crest, Cardinals in Winter, Custard Patterns of Blue Birds, Blue Roses on Blue Satin, Chocolate Roses, Clydesdales, Daisies on Cameo, Frosted Asters, Holly Custard, Pink Blossoms, Sunset, Vintage, and Wildflower.

#7257: 10" Vase. Made in Silver Poppies on Ebony; Satin patterns of Blue Birds; Daisies on Custard; Mountain Reflections; and Roses on Burmese.

#7262: 12" Fan-topped Vase. Made in Silver Jamestown, Apple Blossom, and Silver Crest.

#7300: Fairy Light. Made in virtually in every pattern and treatment by Fenton, from 1970 to present.

#7434: 11" Basket. Made in all Vasa Murrhina colors; Rose Satin.

#7437: 8.5" Basket. Made in all Vasa
Murrhina colors (Mould #6437); 1980s
Overlay colors of Dusty Rose, Federal Blue,
Heritage Green, Periwinkle Blue, &
Candleglow Yellow (Mould #2034); Rose
Satin; Silver Crest, Violets in the Snow;
Spiral Optic in Blue Opalescent & Cameo
Opalescent (Mould #3137); Satin Patterns
of Blue Birds; Daisies on Cameo, Down by
the Station, Log Cabin, Mountain Reflec-
tions, Pink Blossoms, Sunset; Burmese
patterns of Autumn Leaves, Roses on
Burmese, and Scene.

#7451: 6" Vase. Made in Silver Crest; Peach Crest; Rose Satin; Blue Satin; and
Custard; Milk Glass Decorated Patterns of Apple Blossom, Yellow Rose,
Violets in the Snow; Custard patterns of Pink Blossom, Daisies on Custard,
and Red Roses on Custard.

#7453: 8" Vase. Made in Peach Crest; Silver Crest; and all Vasa
Murrhina colors (Mould #6454).

#7457: 5" Vase.
Made in all Vasa
Murrhina colors
(Mould #6465);
and in the Burmese
patterns of Roses on
Burmese, and
Scene.

#7464: Pitcher 16 oz. Made in all Vasa Murrhina colors (Mould #6465): Silver Crest, Violets In the Snow; Country Cranberry (Mould #1866), 1980s Overlay colors of Dusty Rose, Federal Blue, Heritage Green, Periwinkle Blue, & Candleglow Yellow; and Rose Satin.

#7488: Temple Jar. Made in Jade Green; Pekin Blue; Ebony; Amethyst; Decorated patterns of Silver Poppies on Ebony, Blue Dogwood, Blue Garland, Chocolate Roses, Clydesdales, Daisies on Cameo; Dianthus on Custard; Down by the Station; Frosted Asters; Log Cabin; Pink Blossoms; Sunset; Wild Flowers; Vintage; and Sand Carved Iris on Amethyst.

#7468: Cruet. Made in Burmese Satin; Roses on Burmese: Autumn Leaves on Burmese; Blue Opalescent; Cranberry; Topaz Opalescent; French Opalescent Coin Dot (Mould #1473); Polka Dot (Mould #2262); Ruby Overlay Small Dot Optic & Jamestown Transparent (Mould #2473).

#7564: Bell. Made in virtually every treatment, pattern, and color Fenton produced from 1970-85.

#9055: 5" Ribbed Vase. Made in Peach Crest, Jamestown Blue; Spiral Optic in Cranberry Opalescent, Country Cranberry, Burmese, and Blue Burmese.

Items from Fenton Regular Lines That Are Considered Rare, Scarce, & Hard to Find

The following listing contains items that, although in Fenton catalogs and price listings, are hard to find (HTF), scarce, or rare. This listing was compiled by consulting many dealers, and collectors who specialize in Fenton from the 1940 through 1990 time period. Some of the reasons for these items being rare and scarce include: a short issue, problems in making the treatment or item, or the lack of demand for an certain item because of shape, color, or treatment. The items in the following list are considered prizes in any Fenton collection. Most of these items have been pictured previously in *The Big Book of Fenton Glass* and each *Fenton Glass Compendium*.

Coin Dot: Blue Opalescent: Basket 12" 1353; Basket 13" 1523; Candy Dish #93; Cruet #1473; Creamer/Sugar #1924; Decanter #894; Covered Jar #893; 8" #194 2-handled Vase; Any 13" #194 Vases; #894 10" Bottle Shaped Vase.

Coin Dot: Cranberry: Basket 12" 1353; Basket 13" 1523; Candy Dish #93; Creamer/Sugar #1924; Decanter #894; Covered Jar #893; Hurricane Lamps #170; Any 13" #194 Vases; #894 10" Bottle Shaped Vase; HTF items include: Candle Sticks 1470; Handled Bottle 8" #1469.

Coin Dot: French Opalescent: Basket 12" 1353; Basket 13" 1523; Candy Dish #93; Creamer/Sugar #1924; Decanter #894; Covered Jar #893; Any 13" #194 Vases; #894 10" Bottle Shaped Vase.

Coin Dot: Honeysuckle Opalescent: Water Pitchers #1353, both Ruffled and Ice Lipped; Basket #203 7"; Basket 7" 1925.

Coin Dot: Lime Opalescent: Basket 7" #1437; Candy #1522; Vase 11" #1451.

Coin Dot: Topaz Opalescent: Basket 7" 1437; Cruet #1473; Vase 11" #1451; Vase 10" #1442.

Apple Blossom: Epergne 7308; Vase 12" Fan Topped 7262; HTF: Cake Plate 7213.

Aqua Crest: Basket Special #203; Creamer and Basket Minis #37; Any 192 Cologne Bottles, Candies, and Powders with the Hobnail Finials/Stoppers; Candy Covered, Ftd. #206; Hand Vase 10.5" #193.

Emerald Crest: Basket 7" #711; either Epergne; Bowl, Ftd. Square 7330; Mustards on Stand; HTF: Heart Relish #7333; Cake Plate, Low Ftd. #5813.

Flame Crest: Cake Plate #7312; Candlestick 6" #7474.

Gold Crest: Tall Melon Candlesticks #192.

Ivory Crest: Candlesticks #1523; Candlesticks, Ftd. #36.

Peach Crest: Any #711 Vanity Items; #711 Candy; #1353 70 oz Jug; Special Basket #203; Hurricane Lamp #170; Squat Jug #192; Creamer #711; Creamer #192; Hand Vase 10.5" #193.

Black Rose: Basket 7" 7237; Lamp, Hurricane 7398; Hand Vase 10.5 #5155.

Rose Crest: Basket 13" 1523; Candlesticks #1523; Basket, special #203; Cup/saucer.

Snow Crest: All Colors: Any 12" Top Hats; Blue Snow Crest: Any Item.

Hobnail: Blue: Basket 13.5" Made from 8" Flip Vase; Any Square Item; Both the Handled and Plain Punch Bowls; Butter #3977; Melon Ribbed Covered Candy; Cookie Jar; Peg Vase for 1 Horn Epergne; Bottle #3986; Covered Jar; 3 Part Cloverleaf Relish and undivided Relish #3822; 16 oz. Tumbler #3846; Tankard Jug; 6" Hand Vase; 3" Rose Bowl; Decanter w/ Blue Handle & Stopper; 8" Flip Vases, both Cylinder and Cupped in; and 10" Bottle Vase.

Hobnail: Cranberry: Basket 13.5" Made from 8" Flip Vase; Tankard Jug; 3" Rose Bowl; 7" Deep Basket #3637; Mini Sugar/Creamer; Star Crimped Sugar/Creamer; 8" Flared Vase; 10" Bottle Shaped Vase; Covered Jar; 4.5" Ruffled Mini Fan Vase; 8" Flip Vases, both Cylinder and Cupped in.

Hobnail: French Opalescent: Basket 13.5" Made from 8" Flip Vase; Any Square Item; Butter #3977; Melon Ribbed Covered Candy; Cookie Jar; Peg Vase for 1 Horn Epergne; Bottle #3986; Covered Jar; 3 Part Cloverleaf Relish and Undivided Relish #3822; 16 oz. Tumbler #3846; Tankard Jug; 6" Hand Vase; 3" Rose Bowl; Handled Punch Bowl; Decanter; 8" Flip Vases, both Cylinder and Cupped in.

Hobnail: Green (1940s): Vanity Set; Tankard Jug; Squat Jug; Cruet.

Hobnail: Lime Opalescent: Cruet #3863; 4.5" Basket #3834; Vase 9" 3859.

Hobnail: Plum Opalescent: Basket 12" Oval #3839; Epergne #3801; Decanter #3761; Levay Items (1980s): Basket 12" DC 3734; 3 pc. Fairy Light 3804; Heart Relish 3733; Epergne #3701; Pitcher 70 oz. #3664; Pitcher Made from 11" Vase #3306; Wine Goblet #3843 HTF.

Hobnail: Topaz: Basket 13.5" Made from 8" Flip Vase; Melon Ribbed Covered Candy; Cookie Jar; Peg Vase for 1 Horn Epergne; Covered Jar; Tankard Jug; 6"

Hand Vase; Decanter; 80 oz. Jug; 12" Basket #3734; Hanging Bowl #3705; 3 Ftd. Bowl 8.5" #3724; Levay Items (1980s): Butter/Cheese #3677; Banana Boat #3720; HTF: Mini Fan Vase w/Ruffled Top; Cruet; Plate 8" Salad w/Ruffle; Crescent Plate.

Cactus: Topaz Opalescent: Any Baskets; Bowl 8" Ftd. #3422; Banana Bowl #3425; Plate Ftd. #3412; Fan Vase #3489; Cookie Jar #3480; Epergne #3401; Bowl Ftd. #3422.

New World: Any Item in Lime or Dusk; Sugar/Creamer; Goblet; any plates or bowls in Cranberry.

Polka Dot: Cranberry: Butter #2277; Basket 7" #2237; Pitcher 70 oz. #2267; Vase shaped like Pitcher 8" #2259; HTF: Ivy Ball #2221.

Satin Opalescent: Cruets in any colors in Fern Optic, Diamond Optic, or Rib Optic; Anything in Swirled Feather; Anything in any of the patterns in the glossy finish.

Spiral Optic: Any Color: Any 1921 or 1920 Top Hats; Ice Lipped Pitcher, in any color; 1924/1923/1922/1921/1920 Hat Baskets in Any color; Decanter; Covered Rose Jar.

Blue, Green, Ivy, Amber, Gold Overlay: The following items in the #711 Beaded Melon Mould: 10 Basket, Covered Candy, any Vanity Item, Squat Jug, or Creamer; 8" Jug; 8" Vase also in Green and Ivy Overlay 1924; Creamer, 1925; 7" Basket.

Goldenrod: Anything.

Plated Amberina: Basket, Deep 7" #1637; Candy, covered #1680; #1690 Lamp.

Opaque Blue: Wheat Vase #5858; Wave Crest Box #6080; #1690 Lamp.

Mulberry Overlay: Hand Vase #193; #203 7" Basket; #192 10" Basket; #1924 5" Basket; Vanity Set; #1353 Jug; #1353 8" Vase (Shaped Like Jug).

Ruby Overlay in Thumbprint Optic: #1924 7" Basket; Pitcher, 2 qt. #2467; Tumbler, 12 oz. #2447.

Vasa Murrhina: All Colors: Pitcher 6465; Vase 14" 6459.

Block & Star: Turquoise Pastel: Pitcher #5667; Buffet Set #5602.

Lamb's Tongue: Any item in Rose Pastel; Oil Bottle in any color.

Jonquil Yellow: Any item.

Blue Satin: Jefferson Comport; HTF: Grape & Cable Tobacco Jar.

Green Satin: HTF: Grape & Cable Tobacco Jar.

Ebony Crest: #7213; Cake Plate, #7294; Tiered Tidbit; Candle Sticks #7271; #7237 7" Basket.

Apple Blossom on Silver Crest: Basket 5" #7436.

Blue Bells on Hobnail: Basket, Oval 12" 3839; Covered Butterfly Candy, #3600; Fan Vase 8" #3852. All the rest is HTF.

Blue Dogwoods on Cameo Satin: Any 5 petal item.

Clydesdales: Any 2nd series (Opal w/Cameo Blush) items.

Frosted Asters: Candle Light.

Ruby Hobnail: Egg Cup.

Thumbprint: Any Color: Butter Dish #4477; Royal Wedding Bowl #4488.

Rosalene: Praying Children #5100; Fan Vase #8425.

Roses on Burmese: Candy Box #7284; HTF: Basket 7" "Deep" #7238; Vase 11" #7251.

Hanging Hearts: Custard/Turquoise: Barber Bottle #8960; Bottle #8961; Cruet #8969.

Rose Quartz Vase w/Young Lady sandblasted: Connoisseur Collection, 1983.

Animals/Figurals: Ebony Praying Children #5100; Rosalene Praying Children #5100; Lavender Satin Praying Children #5100; Donkey/Cart #5125/5124; Blue Satin Elephant (Trunk Down/Work Elephant) #5108; Donkey/Cart #5125/5124; Violets in the Snow Frog #5166; Red Slag Alley Cat #5177.

Coin Dot - Blue Opalescent - Oil Lamp, late 1940s: This lamp was fashioned from an Atomizer Bottle, which was produced by Fenton for DeVilBiss of Toledo, Ohio. It is unknown what year this shape was actually produced for DeVilBiss, or who took this shape and adapted it into a lamp. I'm certain that these are not "homemade" items as I have seen several with the exact same fitting. VALUE: $125-$150. *Courtesy of Twins Antiques.*

Coin Dot - Blue Opalescent - One Horn Epergne #1522/#1524, 1947: This item was actually listed in the 1947 Fenton catalog and was either discontinued before the catalog came out or shortly afterwards. The price for the horn & frog in Blue and French Opalescent was $9.00 per dozen and in Cranberry it was $12.00 per dozen. According to Frank Fenton, there were production problems in the making of the horn, so it's not known if the horn every reached production or not. VALUE: UND. *Courtesy of Eileen & Dale Robinson.*

As one can see from this picture, the epergne consists of the #1522 10" Bowl, a Crystal Frog, and the #1524 Epergne Vase, which was called a Peg Vase. Both the Frog and Bowl are common; it is the Peg Vase which makes it a rarity! *Courtesy of Eileen & Dale Robinson.*

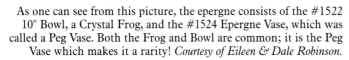

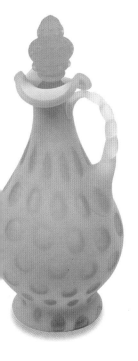

Coin Dot - Blue Opalescent Satin - #894 Decanter, circa 1948: Keep in mind that Fenton had no Opalescent satin items in their regular line until 1953, when Fern, Diamond, Rib Optic, and Swirled Feather was introduced. At times before 1953, items would be satinized, either by special order for another company or if the item had a small imperfection in it. The satinization process would cover a flaw, allowing the satinized flawed piece to be sold. (Remember, the Gift shop did not open until the late 1950s, and they had no other way to cover the expense of these items.) Also keep in mind that now items in the Satin finish by L. G. Wright are much more prized, in some cases, than the glossy finish. A lot of Fenton collectors feel the same way about Satin items made by Fenton. This is ironic. In general glass collecting terms twenty years ago, when I first started in antiques, Satin Glass items, especially Depression glass, were generally looked down upon and not considered collectible! VALUE: $500-$550. *Courtesy of Emogene Snyder.*

Coin Dot - Blue Opalescent - #894 8" Jug Whimsey, late 1940s: This whimsey is pictured next to the Regular Decanter to prove that this unique jug was actually fashioned from that mould. Whether it was made as a sample, to later put into actual production, or was made by a worker on his own time is not known; but, it is a unique piece. VALUE: UND. *Courtesy of Alice & James Rose.*

Coin Dot - Blue Opalescent - Hanging Lamps #1429, circa 1960s: Very unusual item, as most of the hanging lamps were on the teardrop mould. According to the owner of this lamp, most of the examples made in this shape were distributed in the western states. VALUE: $250-$300.

Coin Dot - Blue Opalescent - #194 13" Handled Vase, late 1940s: When first looking at this massive item, you would say that it is the regular 13" handled vase, until you noticed the crimp, which is called the straight edge crimp. Made as a sample item or by a worker as a Whimsey. VALUE: UND. *Courtesy of Betty & Ike Hardman.*

Coin Dot - Blue Opalescent - #1466 7"
Ring Neck Vase Whimsey/#1924 4" Flared
Straight Edge Vase: The #1466 7" Ring
Neck Vase is obviously a Whimsey, an
item that Frank Fenton refers to as
"Walking out in someone's lunch box."
This item was made during the production
of the regular 6" Ring Neck Vase from
1960-61. The #1924 4" Vase with the flared
straight edge could have been produced in
limited quantities, as that crimp had been
somewhat regularly used in the late 1930s
and early 1940s on lines such as Blue
Ridge and the Opalescent Spiral Optic
line. However, this line had been discontinued for some time when Coin Dot was
introduced in 1947. Actually, this is the
simplest of all crimps to produce as this
crimp is what the finisher has to work
with before the actual crimp is made!
VALUE: UND. *Courtesy of Betty & Ike
Hardman.*

Coin Dot - Blue Opalescent - #1353 10" Vase, late 1940s: Made on the
same mould as the 8" #1353 Vase, this vase is taller and has a wider
diameter. It's not known whether this was an item that was to be put into
actual production; but, as this is a complete variation of the #1353 mould,
it's likely that it was. VALUE: UND. *Courtesy of Ike & Betty Hardman.*

Coin Dot - Blue Opalescent - #1472 6" Vase: Although listed in the 1960 Fenton catalog,
little vase seldom pops up at any time. An exact copy of the #1476 8" Vase was also made
Cranberry. VALUE: $90-$110. *Courtesy of Dorothy Hines.*

Coin Dot - Cranberry - #1353 13" Basket, 1947: This is one item that (although it was in the regular Fenton line) is very rare . . . to the point of virtual non-existence! Most serious Cranberry and Coin Dot collectors have not found this prize. Made for less than a year before being discontinued, it's likely that very few of the ones that were sold have survived. In a very ironic twist, in a conversation with a former Fenton employee, who worked in the factory during the 1950s, I found out that most of the large items in all colors of Coin Dot did not sell. When he came to work in the early 1950s, it was one of his jobs to make more room for updating the factory. To accomplish this, the unsold items in Coin Dot were broken, dumped, and buried in a lot behind the Fenton factory. If he hadn't mentioned that they had been broken, I would have been out there with a shovel myself! VALUE: $900-$1,000. *Courtesy of Emogene Snyder.*

Coin Dot - Cranberry - Epergne One Horn #1522/1524, 1947: This piece could be considered one of the rarest of the rare! Consisting of the #1522 10" Bowl and #1524 Peg Vase, it was made only for a short time in 1947. It is confirmed that it was made in Blue Opalescent and is suspected to exist in French Opalescent. The Cranberry would be considered to be the most in demand. I have confirmed, so far, that five exist in carefully guarded collections. According to Frank Fenton, the Peg Vase was difficult to produce. For that reason, it was quickly discontinued. VALUE: UND. *Courtesy of Eileen & Dale Robinson.*

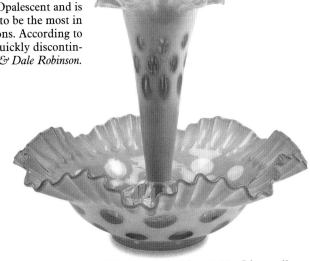

Coin Dot - Cranberry - Decorated #92 Dresser Set, late 1940s: It's a well known fact that many different items produced by Fenton through the 1940s were sold to, and decorated by, Abels Wasserberg; but, it is surprising to know that a few in Coin Dot, and especially in Cranberry Dot, were decorated with Abels Wasserberg's "Charleton" Flowers. VALUE: $550-$600. *Courtesy of John & Linda Flippen.*

Coin Dot - Cranberry - Large Candy/#203 7" Basket, late 1940s: This candy is somewhat larger than the regular #1522, but has a smaller opening for the lid. The opening accepts the #91 Candy Dish Lid. Again, this had to have been a sample item, as the mould is completely different than what has ever been recorded. The #203 7" Basket with the straight edge was in all probability made in the late 1940s with the straight edge crimp. Again, it was produced early in the Coin Dot run as an sample to test market appeal, or was produced as a worker's Whimsey. VALUE: UND. *Courtesy of John & Linda Flippen.*

Coin Dot- Cranberry - Decorated #814 Handled Bottle/#1924 4" Top Hat/#203 5" Vase, late 1940s: Items produced by Fenton, decorated by Abels Wasserberg. VALUE: #814 Handled Bottle: $550-$650; Top Hat: $125-$150; 5" Vase: $325-$375. *Courtesy of John & Linda Flippen.*

Coin Dot - Cranberry - Decorated 189 10" Vase, late 1940s: A different type of decoration than pictured on the previous items with no label or markings, which makes positively identifying this as Abels Wasserberg almost impossible; but, with the type of flowers being the same as the ones on Cambridge Crown Tuscan, it is fairly likely. VALUE: $375-$425. *Courtesy of Emogene Snyder.*

Coin Dot - Cranberry - Small Ginger Jar: This item was originally produced as a lamp fount, and usually has the bottom drilled out to run the cord through. But in this particular case, the bottom has not been drilled, nor is there the usual indentation for positioning the drill. I found this item, without the lid, around 15 years ago at a small rural auction. Later, I discovered that the lid to the small Wrisley French Opal Hobnail Ginger Jar fits it, and have displayed them together since that time. This is the only example that I have ever seen produced without the indent for drilling the hole to accept the lamp cord. 5" tall, 4" diameter. VALUE: UND. *Author's Collection.*

Coin Dot - Cranberry - #1721 Pinched Decanter - Rose Bowl from a #1522 Candy Bottom, circa early 1950s: Two very unusual items that were never in Fenton's regular Coin Dot line. At first glance, the Rose Bowl looks to be the regular #1522 Candy Bottom; but, upon closer examination, you will observe that the top flares out farther than the candy bottom and it also has a slight rim at the top of the piece. VALUE: UND.

Coin Dot - Cranberry - #1425 4" Rose Bowl with Straight Edge, circa late 1950s: Made off the #1425 4" Rose Bowl. Either this was a Whimsey the finisher did not crimp or Fenton sampled this item for a different shape of rose bowl. Whichever the case, it is a very unusual item. VALUE: UND. *Courtesy of Linda and John Flippen.*

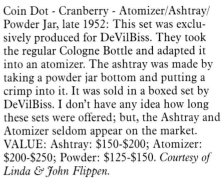

Coin Dot - Cranberry - Atomizer/Ashtray/Powder Jar, late 1952: This set was exclusively produced for DeVilBiss. They took the regular Cologne Bottle and adapted it into an atomizer. The ashtray was made by taking a powder jar bottom and putting a crimp into it. It was sold in a boxed set by DeVilBiss. I don't have any idea how long these sets were offered; but, the Ashtray and Atomizer seldom appear on the market. VALUE: Ashtray: $150-$200; Atomizer: $200-$250; Powder: $125-$150. *Courtesy of Linda & John Flippen.*

Coin Dot - Cranberry - Cigarette Lighter, circa 1960s: This is a unique item. I honestly don't know if it was a special order piece, made from the bottom of the #1457 7.5" Vase, or if someone cut the top off of the vase and then fit the lighter into it. Whichever the case, it is a nicely made and finished item. VALUE: UND. *Courtesy of Linda & John Flippen.*

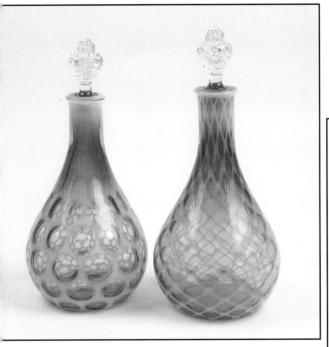

Coin Dot/Diamond Optic - Cranberry - Wine Bottles, late 1940s?: Made from the #894 Mould, a plunger was place in the bottom of the mould so that this item would come out without a foot. Then it was finished off without a handle, and with a straight edge, making both of these bottles look quite different from the regular #894 Decanter. These were possibly produced as sample items. Unfortunately, they were never placed into regular production. VALUE: UND. *Courtesy of Eileen & Dale Robinson.*

Coin Dot - Cranberry Satin - #894 Decanter: It's hard to date any of Fenton's Satin items, as most items produced were made at different times throughout the regular run of an item. As I stated before, it is difficult to know if a Satin piece was made for another company to sell or if the satinizing process was employed to hide a flaw in the glass. VALUE: UND. *Courtesy of Audrey & Joe Elsinger.*

Coin Dot – Cranberry (CRN)/French Opalescent (FO) - #814 8" Bottle, late 1940s: When the Cranberry Bottle was first pictured in the *Big Book of Fenton Glass 1940-70,* it was assumed, with the absence of the spout and handle from the regular #1469 Bottle, that this was a Whimsey. Now that an example has appeared in French Opalescent, it's more likely that these bottles were sampled in different colors. VALUE: CRN: $600-$700; FO: $500-$600. *Courtesy of John & Linda Flippen.*

Coin Dot - Cranberry - Dresser Bottle, circa late 1940s: In the making of this book, I would write the descriptions of different items as I took the pictures, so the previous items and the ones appearing after this item may have actually been completed some months before this shot was taken and item described. In this case, the photo for this bottle was taken about a month before the completion of this book. As I have stated many times, never think that you know everything about a certain pattern, and what there is in it! It's uncertain what mould that this piece was made from. VALUE: UND. *Courtesy of Linda Flippen and John Flippen.*

Coin Dot - Cranberry - Dresser Bottle: Notice the ground top of the bottle, which is Unique for Fenton . . . and most other companies of this type!

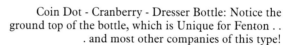

Coin Dot - Cranberry - Dresser Bottle: L to R: #814 Handless Bottle, #1465 Cologne, Unlisted Dresser Bottle, #208 Cruet. Notice the difference in shape and size between the unlisted Dresser Bottle and the other bottles! L to R: $600-$700; $125-150; UND; $275-$300. *Courtesy of Linda and John Flippen.*

Coin Dot - Cranberry - #1925 6" Scalloped Edge Jug, late1940s?: This item is very much classified as a Whimsey, where they took a regular 6" Vase, added a handle, applied A unique Scalloped Crimp, and spout, and made a pitcher. VALUE: UND. *Courtesy of John & Linda Flippen.*

Coin Dot - Cranberry - Whimsey Creamer/#180 Hyacinth Vase, late 1940s: The creamer is an exceptionally unusual item made from the #203 Vase. Another example from this same mould in Rose Overlay is also pictured in this book. The #180 Hyacinth Vase, in Cranberry Coin Dot, was probably the most unusual and overlooked item that appeared in the *Big Book of Fenton Glass 1940-70.* It was common, at that time, and even now, for Fenton to take a mould that had been in retirement for several years and reuse it in a completely different pattern, treatment, or color. The Hyacinth Vase was made during the 1930s, mostly in the Satin Etch treatments, and has not been used since that time. It might be noted that, in a recent seminar, George and Nancy Fenton mention that many of the Moulds owned by the Fenton Company have now been catalogued and are hoped to be put back into production. Some of these moulds had been retired since the 1920s and 1930s. VALUE: UND. *Courtesy of Betty & Ike Hardman.*

Coin Dot - Cranberry - 18" Lamp, mid-1960s: Made for the Ruby Company by Fenton. At this time, Fenton made only the glass part of a lamp, and another company would buy the parts, and assemble the lamp. Fenton did not start assembling their own lamps until the mid-to-late 1960s. You might keep in mind that the glass pieces in this lamp were made from the #183 Vase Mould, so it may be possible that a Coin Dot Vase could also exist in this shape! VALUE: $450-$550. *Courtesy of John & Linda Flippen.*

Coin Dot - Cranberry - Candlesticks with Marble Bases and Brass Holders, late 1940s: This pair makes a good example of an item assembled from parts by more than one company. Fenton produces a piece of glass as a lamp component, for example, and another company buys it and transforms the glass piece into a candlestick with the addition of parts of their own manufacture. The Coin Dot pieces pictured here were originally made to be Lamp Globes (*see* the oil lamp in the Dot Optic Section). They were fashioned from the body of the #194 6" Vase. Another company bought them from Fenton and fitted the brass and marble parts onto them, making the candleholders. This was a common practice during this time period. VALUE: UND. *Courtesy of Janice & Gordy Bowerman.*

Coin Dot - Cranberry - #1925 11" Lamp, circa late 1940s: Unique item made for the Max Horn, Zermer & Lewis Company. I have also seen this shape in Ruby Snow Crest with Abels Wasserberg Charleton Flowers. VALUE: UND. *Courtesy of Emogene Snyder.*

Coin Dot - 16" Cranberry Lamp, circa late 1950s: This lamp is one of several, that appears from time to time, that was fashioned from glass pieces which were offered in Fenton's Lamp Parts catalogs in the late 1950s and early 1960s. These glass pieces would be bought by other individuals/companies and made up using their own metal fittings. VALUE: $300+. *Courtesy of Linda and John Flippen.*

Coin Dot - Cranberry - 32" Lamp: I mentioned in the *Big Book of Fenton Glass*, that I did not include lamps made in the 1940-70 time period as they were assembled by other companies. I did catch some fire for that; I also received requests that I do a book solely on lamps, which would be virtually impossible, as this book shows. You can virtually take any item that Fenton adapted to drill a hole into and make a lamp from it. Many companies, as in the same case of L. G. Wright, did exactly that. You could go to their assembly facility and make up your own lamp, from whatever pieces they had available. That is why so many unusual lamps pop up. I have also seen other items besides lamps made from Fenton glass parts, including several French Opalescent Coin Dot Floor Ashtrays which incorporated the #894 Decanter vase as the stem and the #1522 Candy Bottom as the ash receiver, with a metal lid which held the Ashtray. All of these Ashtrays have appeared in the central Indiana area, so some company from that area must have made them to order. VALUE: UND. *Courtesy of Emogene Snyder.*

Cranberry Coin Dot - 22" Lamp, circa 1940s-50s. VALUE: $350-$450. *Courtesy of Emogene Snyder.*

Cranberry Coin Dot - 30"
Lamp, circa 1940s-50s:
Assembled by the Armslay
Lamp Company in the late
1950s. VALUE: $450-$550.
Courtesy of Emogene Snyder.

Cranberry - Coin Dot - 25"
Gone with the Wind (GWTW)
Lamp, circa 1950s: A truly
massive item, and very scarce.
The glass parts were pictured
in a mid-1950s Fenton catalog
that catered to the lamp trade.
VALUE: $500-$600. *Courtesy
of Emogene Snyder.*

Cranberry - Coin Dot -
Hanging Lamp, circa 1960s:
Same shape as the Blue
Opalescent example pictured
previously. With both this
color and Blue appearing, it
would be safe to say that these
lamps were made close to
1959-61, when Fenton again
was producing Blue Opalescent, after it had been discontinued in 1956. VALUE: $450-
$550.

Coin Dot - Cranberry - Mini Lamp "Alice Minister Originals,"
circa 1950s?: Unique little item, fashioned from the Cologne
bottle and what has been referred to as the Coin Dot Nut Dish.
Keep in mind that, although this Nut Dish/Shade looks like the
7" Bowl, it is only 4.5" in diameter. Now to find the regular Nut
Dish!! VALUE: UND. *Courtesy of Linda and John Flippen.*

Coin Dot

Coin Dot - Cranberry Mini Lamp, circa 1950s: Unique shape made from the cologne bottle and the middle of a 6" #194 vase. VALUE: UND. *Courtesy of Emogene Snyder.*

Coin Dot - French Opalescent (FO) - #89▮ Vase, 1947-49: Although in Fenton's regula▮ line for several years, just try to find this vase in Coin Dot in any color! VALUE: FO: $200-$250.

Coin Dot - Cranberry - #898 11" Vase: This mould had been in use by Fenton for some years during the 1920s and 1930s. It appeared more frequently in 1961, in use with the 1960s overlay colors in Bubble Optic, and has been used periodically since that time. The first time it was used in regular production was in Spiral Optic, in Cranberry, in 1956. Before that, it had not appeared in any Fenton line since the mid-1930s. Although it is known in Cranberry Dot Optic and now in Coin Dot, this one, for the collector of Coin Dot, is a "must" on their want list! VALUE: $450-$550. *Courtesy of Emogene Snyder.*

Coin Dot - Honeysuckle Opalescent - #1450 5" Vase, circa mid-1950s: Although this shape was in the regular line in Honeysuckle in 1948, this vase is much darker than the regular 1948 issue. Actually, this is the same shade of Honeysuckle that was used in the late 1950s and on into the 1960s, while Fenton produced Lamps for other companies. It was probable that, sometime during the 1950s, Honeysuckle was a color in consideration to be reissued and was sampled. Items known to have been produced in this later run of Honeysuckle include this piece, the Coin Dot 6" #1466 Ring Neck Vase, and the 11" #1452 Vase pictured next. VALUE: UND.

Coin Dot - Honeysuckle Opalescent - #1452 11" Vase, circa 1952-61: This shape in Coin Dot was in use by Fenton during the 1950s. It was produced in Cranberry and Lime Opalescent in Fenton's regular line. Fenton's actual Honeysuckle color had been discontinued several years before this mould was in production. Also, as with the 5" Vase pictured previously, it's much darker than the regular issue of Honeysuckle Opalescent of 1948. VALUE: UND. *Courtesy of Sharen and Al Creery.*

Coin Dot - Honeysuckle Opalescent - Large and Small Colonial Lamps, 1950s and 1960s: Although Honeysuckle Opalescent was discontinued in the late 1940s, Fenton continued to produced lamp parts for other companies in this color. Later, in the early 1960s, when Fenton started its Lamp Division, Honeysuckle Coin Dot was produced in Lamp parts, along with other items. It is hard to tell if these lamps were made in the 1950s or in the 1960s. VALUE: Small Lamp: $250-$300; Large Lamp: $300-$400. *Courtesy of Betty & Ike Hardman.*

Coin Dot - Lime Opalescent/Cranberry - #1522 Candy Dishes with Brass Lids, circa 1953-54: Another item for which Fenton was responsible for the glass part, which they sold to another company, who fitted it with the brass cover studded with Rhinestones and fitted with a marble finial. VALUE: UND. *Courtesy of Janice & Gordy Bowerman.*

Coin Dot - Lime Opalescent - Ivy Ball on Green Diamond Stand, circa 1953: Lime Opalescent in Coin Dot was introduced into the Fenton Line in 1953 and Ivy Balls on Diamond Bases were in production at around the same time. Obviously, it was during this time period that this piece was produced, probably as a sample item. VALUE: UND. *Courtesy of Betty & Ike Hardman.*

Coin Dot - Lime Opalescent - #894 10" Vase, mid-1950s?: It's hard to tell when this item was made by Fenton, as the #894 10" Vase had been discontinued for at least 4 years before Lime Opalescent came into the Fenton Line. According to Frank Fenton, it might of been made as a special order for H.A. Framburg of Chicago. VALUE: UND. *Courtesy of Betty & Ike Hardman.*

Coin Dot - Lime Opalescent - #194 13" Vase, circa 1953: When this vase, along with its mate, appeared on eBay, it unnerved everyone who thought they knew about Fenton! I have already confirmed that the #194 shape vases exist in the 6" (shown) and 8" sizes in my previous books. With the appearance of the 13" vase, it's possible that an 11" vase also exists. I have also confirmed the existence of a pair of Lime Opalescent Coin Dot Lamps made from the 1 handled 8" Vase. To top off the whole matter, those lamps are decorated with the Abels Wasserberg "Charleton" Flowers! VALUE: UND. *Courtesy of Audrey and Joe Elsinger.*

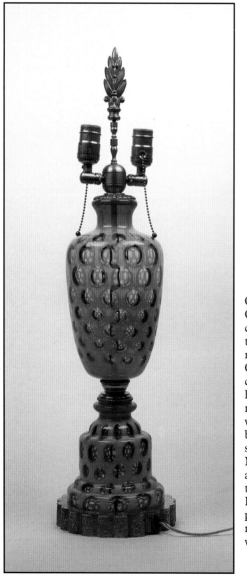

Coin Dot - Lime Opalescent - Lamp, circa 1950s: I have seen this *shape* of lamp many times in French Opalescent; however, I could not quite honestly convince myself that this lamp was made by Fenton because of the unusual shape of the two *founts*. Now that it has appeared in this color, there is no doubt that Fenton made it! In person, this lamp is marvelous beyond words. VALUE: UND.

Coin Dot - Orange Opalescent - #7451 6" Melon Ribbed Vase, mid-1960s: Obviously Colonial Orange cased with Opal. Because of the time frame in which Colonial Orange was made, this vase and a few other shapes had to have been sampled in the mid-1960s. VALUE: UND.

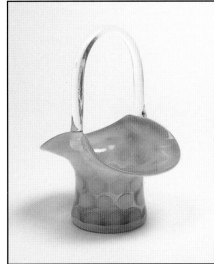

Dot Optic - Cranberry - #1924 5" Smooth Edge Basket, circa 1940s: I have never figured why a certain item will look so strange when it is crimped differently than it is regularly. VALUE: $150-$175. *Courtesy of Linda & John Flippen.*

Dot Optic - Blue Opalescent - #1522 10" Basket, circa early 1940s: At the time that I compiled the listing of items for the Dot Optic section in the *Fenton Glass Compendium*, I thought I had covered everything that had been confirmed to exist, or could exist, in that pattern. How wrong I was! It seems that every time I'm out at a show or on a buying trip, I find another piece in this pattern! With the appearance of this basket in both Blue and Topaz Opalescent, it is a good possibility that it also exists in Cranberry and, possibly, French Opalescent. VALUE: $200+. *Courtesy of Barbara Ryley.*

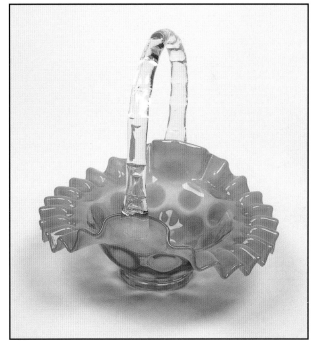

Dot Optic - Cranberry - #203 7" Basket : Made for the J. Willfred Co. in 1946. Later in the 1940s, baskets in this shape and size became a Fenton mainstay in their regular lines. VALUE: $175-$200. *Courtesy of Audrey and Joe Elsinger.*

Dot Optic - Topaz Opalescent - #1522 10" Basket/ #1353 10" Basket, circa early 1940s: It never has been certain when Fenton produced the Dot Optic pattern—or if it wasn't produced mostly by them for other companies—due to a lack of accurate records from that time at the factory. Frank Fenton has confirmed that the #203 7" Basket, pictured here, was made for J. Willfred Co. in 1946. Whether the pattern was in full production at that time is uncertain. I'm believe, from looking over the past few years at the shapes and colors that Dot Optic has appeared in, that it was probably introduced in 1938-39 (at the same time that Spiral Optic was in production) and remained in production until at least 1941, when Topaz Opalescent was being made by Fenton. Whether this pattern was made solely for other companies or not is still unsure; however, no records of this pattern exist on Fenton price sheets from that time. Both of these baskets are extremely rare, as is most anything in Topaz Dot Optic. The #1353 10" Basket was made off the same mould as the #1353 Jug from that time period. VALUE: #1522 10" Basket: $300+; #1353 10" Basket: UND.

Dot Optic - Cranberry - #1924 4" Top Hat Vase, circa 1940s: Unique crimp, with a smooth edge, and pulled at each side to resemble a fan crimp. VALUE: UND.

Dot Optic - Blue Opalescent - #1924 4" Top Hat/ #1921 9" Top Hat, circa 1940s. VALUE: #1924 4" Top Hat: $100-$125; #1921 9" Top Hat: $300+.

Dot Optic - Cranberry/Blue Opalescent - #1923 Rolled Crimp Creamer, circa late 1930s: Unique crimp, only seen on the Dot Optic #1924 Creamer and the Coin Dot #1924 Creamer. This is possibly a Whimsey, due to this crimp. VALUE: UND. *Courtesy of Alice & James Rose.*

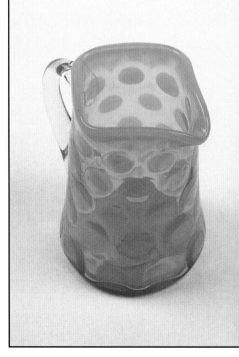

Dot Optic - Blue Opalescent - #1923 Square Top Creamer, circa 1940s: Very unusual crimp on this creamer. This crimp was only used otherwise on the #894 10" Vase in the 1930s, when produced in different Satin Etch patterns and the Blue Ridge Pattern. VALUE: UND. *Courtesy of Judy & Ckriss Cord.*

Dot Optic - Cranberry - #192 Melon Lamp with Coin Dot Shade, circa late 1940s: A unique item made off the #192 Cologne mould. This mould was also used to make Oil Lamps in Ruby Overlay, Mulberry, Blue Overlay, and Rose Overlay. You might keep in mind that no Colognes have ever been reported in Cranberry Dot Optic; but, with the presence of this lamp using the Cologne mould, it's possible that such a Cologne might exist! It's not sure that the shade to this lamp is original, as Coin Dot was not introduced until 1947, some years after this lamp was made. Probably the original shade was a clear glass chimney-type shade. VALUE: UND. *Courtesy of Linda & John Flippen.*

Dot Optic - Amethyst Opalescent - #1353 Jug, circa 1930s. VALUE: $400+.

Dot Optic - French Opalescent - #1355 Tankard Jug, late 1930s: Made on a mould previously used for Fenton's Satin Etch patterns, this item is also unique because of the Ruby handle. VALUE: $400+. *Courtesy of Alice & James Rose.*

Dot Optic - Topaz Opalescent - #203 4" Vase/#201 5" Vase, circa 1940s. VALUE: #203 4" Vase: $150-$200; #201 5" Vase: $250+.

Dot Optic - Blue Opalescent - #894 10" Vase, circa late 1930s- early 1940s: This vase was made from another mould that was in the regular Fenton line at the time that the Dot Optic pattern was produced; however, any vases in this shape are extremely rare in any color. VALUE: $200-$250. *Courtesy of Betty & Ike Hardman.*

Dot Optic - French Opalescent - #898 11" Vase, 1938: While we are most familiar with this shape in Bubble Optic in the 1960s overlay colors and various patterns of Cranberry Opalescent from the past 12 years, many people don't realize that this shape was used many times prior to 1940 by Fenton in several different treatments and after its appearance in Dot Optic in 1938. It was retired for more than 20 years, prior to its use again in the early 1960s. VALUE: $175-$200. *Author's Collection.*

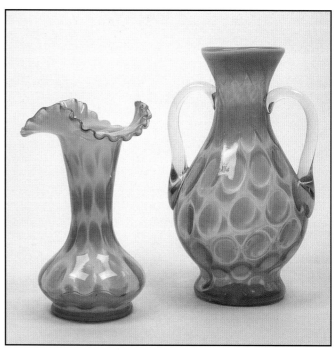

Dot Optic - Blue Opalescent - #894 9" Handled Vase/#186 7" Vase, circa 1940s. VALUE: #894 9" Handled Vase: UND; #186 7" Vase: $110-$125.

Dot Optic - Blue Opalescent - 7" Vase-Unknown Line Number, late 1930s: This same shape was pictured in the Dot Optic section of the *Fenton Glass Compendium 1940-1970* in French Opalescent. Also known in Green Opalescent. We are hopefully waiting for one to appear in Cranberry! VALUE: $65-$85. *Courtesy of Michael and Lori Palmer.*

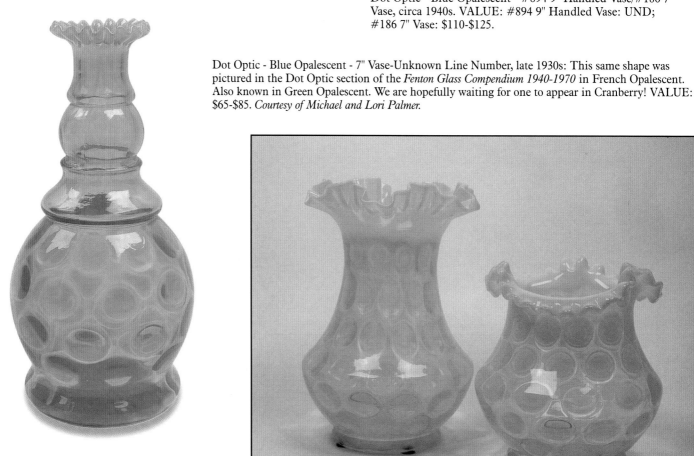

Dot Optic - Topaz Opalescent - #183 6.5" Vase/ #182 9.5" Vase, circa 1940s. VALUE: UND.

Chapter Three
Crests

Aqua Crest - #711 7" Basket, circa 1951: While the Emerald #711 7" Basket was in Fenton's regular line, there are no records of one in Aqua Crest. This is possibly a sample item. Keep in mind that many of the #711 items were very short issue items. VALUE: UND.
Courtesy of Lee Chadwell.

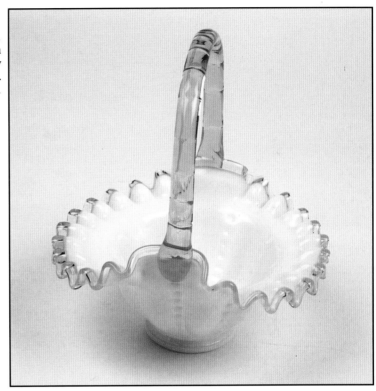

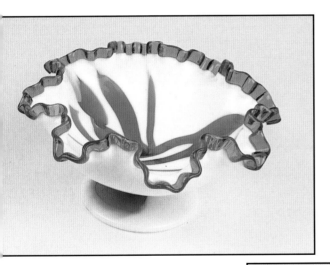

Blue Crest - #7228 Comport with Bird, circa 1963: Probably one of the most unique items in Aqua Crest that has surfaced in the past several years. This comport was designed so that, when it was made, the blue that was gathered with the Milk Glass would settle into the shape of a bird. (Don't even ask me how, just chalk it up to "the magic of making glass!") This is an example of Art Glass at its finest, when someone can take something completely uncontrollable, such as molten Glass, and form it into a pattern like this! VALUE: UND.
Courtesy of Susie, Tiffany, & Ron Ballard.

Blue Crest - #7228 Comport with Bird, circa 1963: close-up of the bird.

Aqua Crest - #1353 13" Bowl with Basket Crimp, circa 1942: Very unusual crimp, usually reserved for items that were to have been produced as Baskets. Some examples do appear, from time to time, without the handle, but not often. VALUE: $125-$150. *Courtesy of Lynne and Gary Virden.*

Aqua Crest - #187 Basket/#1924 Whimsey Creamer with Ice Lip, circa 1942: It is unknown whether the #187 Basket was in Fenton's regular line, due to the almost nonexistent record keeping at the factory at the time. There are several known to exist, so this could be a sample item. The #1924 Creamer with the Ice Lip is too far out, especially when you notice the blue crest applied to the tip of the spout! VALUE: UND. *Courtesy of Alice & James Rose.*

Aqua Crest - Whimsey Mug, circa 1942: Frank Fenton likes to refer to items like this with the phrase, "They took up legs and walked out of the factory." This is a unique item, probably made by a worker in his off time. VALUE: UND. *Courtesy of Betty and Ike Hardman.*

Aqua Crest - #1924 Creamer/ Footed Cup, Creamer circa 1942, Cup circa 1948: It is believed that the #1924 Creamer (notice the difference between this creamer and the previous one) was in the regular line when Aqua Crest began in 1942, but was discontinued shortly after that. The footed cup was the original cup produced in 1948 for the Aqua Crest Dinnerware line. When it proved too costly and difficult to make, this cup was revamped into the flat cup. VALUE: Creamer: $100-$125, Footed Cup: $90-$110. *Courtesy of Lee Chadwell.*

Aqua Crest - Comparison of the footed and flat cup.

Aqua Crest - #680 Creamer and Sugar, 1948: At the same time that the footed cup was produced in Aqua, this sugar and creamer form was in the line. They, like the cup, were soon discontinued and replaced with the Creamer and Sugar commonly seen today. VALUE: UND. *Courtesy of Alice and James Rose.*

Aqua Crest - Unlisted Sugar, circa 1948: Of all the #680 Creamers I have seen, as pictured previously, they were always with a Sugar that looked similar to the Mayonnaise or Deep Dessert Bowl. When I found this Sugar, it was with a Creamer like the one pictured previously and was said to have come out of a former Fenton worker's home. It might have represented one of two things: either the Sugar was made for this worker as a Whimsey, for his own use (and "Walked out of the factory in a lunch box," as Frank Fenton has many times stated of different items), or it was made as a sample item to go along with the #680 Creamer, and it was later decided Fenton would market the Creamer with the Mayonnaise/Deep Dessert Bowl instead. VALUE: UND. *Courtesy of Lee Chadwell.*

Aqua Crest - #192 Oil Lamp: Several times, I have seen this shape with the handle made as Cruets and Lamps in Ruby, Mulberry, Rose, and Blue Overlay. But this piece of Aqua Crest is somewhat different, as it measures approximately 6" tall and 6" in diameter. It completely dwarfs the regular small, squat #192A Cologne, which was usually used to make the oil lamp. VALUE: UND. *Courtesy of Vann Funderburk.*

Aqua Crest - #192 11" Bottle, 1942: With the appearance of this bottle in Aqua Crest, and also Ruby Overlay and Mulberry Overlay, it is quite possible that it may exist in Blue Overlay and Rose Overlay. (For more history on this shape, see the Mulberry Overlay section.) VALUE: UND. *Courtesy of Mary Rimer.*

Blue Crest - Spanish Lace #3537 10" Basket/Spanish Lace #3570 Candlesticks/#7437 Basket, circa late 1960s: It is apparent, with the appearance of these items, that Fenton had thought of reissuing Blue Crest in the late 1960s or early 1970s. You should note that the #7437 Basket shape was later used on such lines as Blue Birds, Violets in the Snow, and Butterflies on Milk Glass. VALUE: Candlesticks: UND; 10" Basket: UND; 7" Basket: UND. *Courtesy of Eileen & Dale Robinson.*

Blue Crest Spanish Lace #3551 8" Vase/Aqua Crest #192 6" Jug with Ruby Handle. Vase, circa late 1960s; Jug, circa early 1940s: The Spanish vase is another of the items that was sampled in the late 1960s, when Fenton considered reissuing Aqua/Blue Crest for the fourth time. It is interesting to note that some of these same pieces were used to make items with a Twilight Blue Crest in the 1990s for QVC! The 6" Jug with the Ruby Handle was made in the early 1940s, either as a special order for another company to sell or as a Whimsey item. VALUE: UND. *Courtesy of Eileen and Dale Robinson.*

Aqua Crystal Crest - 10" Bowl: As Crystal Crest was deemed too difficult to produced in 1942, the same was true for this treatment some years later. It is known that a #7228 Comport also exists in Aqua Crystal Crest. VALUE: UND. *Courtesy of Eileen & Dale Robinson.*

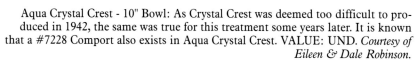

Colonial Green Crest - #7333 Heart Relish, circa mid-1960s: After seeing this item for the first time, it changes my opinion entirely about Colonial Green. Whether it is the Milk Glass that gives it a softer color or the shape that it is on that makes it is more appealing, I don't know; but, it makes for a unique piece. VALUE: UND. *Courtesy of Eileen and Dale Robinson.*

Emerald Crest - Flower Arranger, circa late 1940s: THIS IS NOT THE PRODUCT OF SOME THWARTED GLASS MAKER GONE MAD! This item is what was known in the Victorian time period as a "flower arranger," a predecessor to the popular glass frog that we are now familiar with. This item, produce in Emerald Crest, was probably a Whimsey produced early in the run of Emerald Crest during the late 1940s. VALUE: UND. *Courtesy of Betty & Ike Hardman.*

Emerald Crests/Gold Crest - Oil Bottle/Sugar Bowl: The Oil Bottle in Emerald Crest was produced for the Rubels Company in the mid-1950s. It was made off the Oil Bottle mould that was used for the Emerald Glow items, and has also surfaced in Silver Crest. The Gold Crest Sugar Bowl is virtually unique, as there are only two known to exist, and no creamer with either! It is also ironic that I was making arrangements to take the picture of this one the night that the other known Sugar bowl went off eBay. They both ended up in homes less than seventy miles from each other! VALUE: UND. *Courtesy of Luann and Atlee Beene.*

Flame Crest - 8" Plate/Handled Tray, circa 1963: Both items were usually used in the Tidbit Tray. The plate somehow escaped the drilling process, and the metal handled tray either had been (at one time) part of the Tidbit or sold through the Gift Shop in its present form. VALUES: UND. *Courtesy of Eileen & Dale Robinson.*

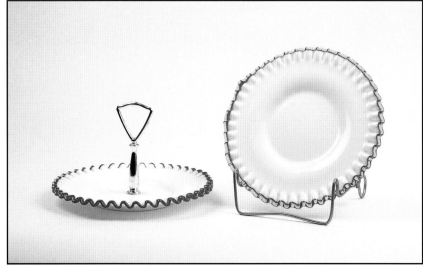

Flame Crest - 12" Plate, circa 1963: Another item that had originally been intended for use as part of the Tidbit but missed the drilling process. VALUE: UND. *Courtesy of Rick and Cindy Blais.*

Flame Crest - #7458 11" Vase, circa 1963: With the Crest line, you will never know what color they will use to ring an item. I have never failed to be surprised when I see a item, normally known in Silver Crest, ringed in a color such as this vase in Flame Crest. In all respects, it could be possible that there are many more Silver Crest shapes in existence that have been made in colors and have found their way out of the factory. VALUE: UND. *Courtesy of Laurie and Richard Karman.*

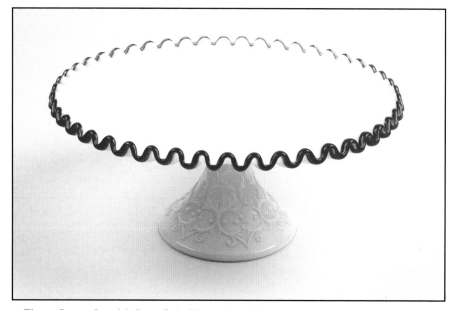

Flame Crest - Spanish Lace Cake Plate, circa 1963: One word can be said for this piece, Beautiful! It puzzles me that Fenton did no produce more items on the Spanish Lace moulds in the colored Crests. This was a sample item. VALUE: UND. *Courtesy of Dale & Eileen Robinson.*

Flame Crest - Spanish Lace Shakers, circa 1963: I get one impression seeing this pair up close, gleaming white rockets about to blast off with a ring of fire encircling their bases! Boy, do I have a wild imagination! VALUE: UND. *Courtesy of Laurie and Richard Karman.*

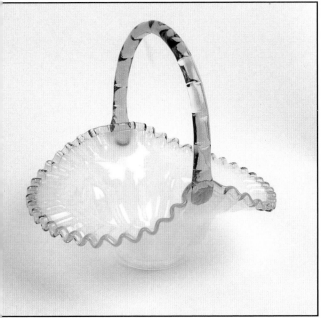

Gold Crest - #192 10" Basket, circa 1943: If you will look close at this basket, and the two in the next picture, you will see a subtle difference in the milk glass—the grayer milk glass is on what Fenton referred to as Opal, and was a predecessor to Milk Glass. It could be that, during the early years of developing Milk Glass, before the Crest line came into being, this item was sampled. VALUE: $150-$175. *Courtesy of JR Antiques.*

Gold Crest - #7339 Divided Basket, circa early 1960s: My first reaction, when I found this piece several years ago, was WOW! It then set me to wondering, since many items in Silver Crest were never made in any of the colored Crest, what else could be out there! This item, again, was another case where the mould was not in current use. It was used to sample a upcoming line, in this case Gold Crest, which was reintroduced into the Fenton line in 1963. VALUE: UND. *Courtesy of Lee Chadwell.*

Gold Crest - 10" Basket - Comparison of the Opal with Gold Crest 10" Basket and the Regular Gold Crest 10" Basket.

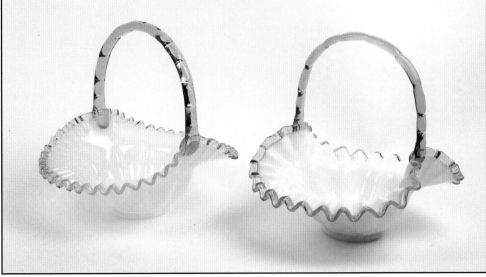

Gold Crest - #192 Powder Jar, circa 1944: At first look, this seems to be a normal powder jar; but, look closely at the lid's round finial instead of the usual melon finial. This was either a Whimsey or a sample item. Keep in mind also that, when Fenton first created the Melon line, they did not use Melon stoppers or finials. They used Hobnail stoppers and finials instead. It must have been extremely short issue, as I have also see the Melon stoppers and finials on Aqua Crest. This goes the same for the overlay colors of Blue, Mulberry, Rose, and Ruby. Both the clear Hobnail stoppers and the lids with the Hobnail finials are correct, besides the regular melon lids. I have seen, in one instance, a Mulberry powder jar pictured with a Hobnail lid and finial. I don't know if this is the right lid for this piece or not, but with Fenton, making the Melon lids with Hobnail finials, and using Hobnail stoppers, they could have also borrowed the Hobnail lids to used on the Melon items. VALUE: UND. *Courtesy of Laurie and Richard Karman.*

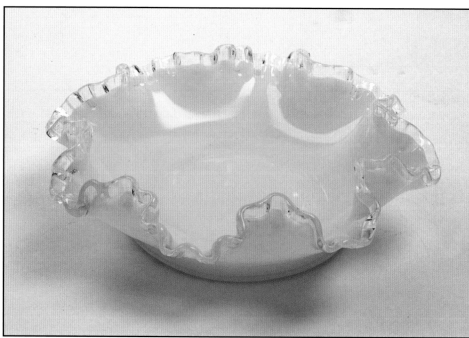

Ivory/Custard Crest - 4" Basket, circa 1970: A special order item marked Fontainebleau on the bottom. The color is similar to Ivory Crest, but is probably Glossy Custard Satin, which was in production at that time. VALUE: UND. *Author's Collection.*

Ivory/Custard Crest - 8" Bowl, circa 1970: Another special order item, this time marked Castlebleu. VALUE: UND. *Courtesy of Lori and Michael Palmer.*

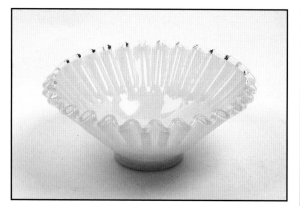

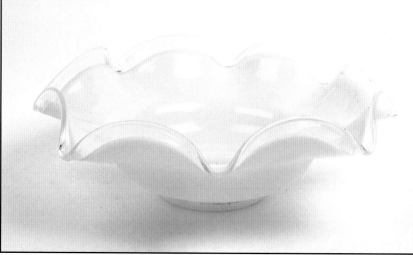

Ivory Crest - 7" Bowl, 1942: Unique flared bowl with a pie crust crimp. VALUE: $65-$75. *Courtesy of Lori and Michael Palmer.*

Ivory Crest - 10" #1522 Bowl, circa 1942: The bowl itself is ordinary, but the crimp is what is the unusual part of this item. Made for a short while, mostly on Silver Crest, this type of crimp has become very popular with Crest collectors. VALUE: $100-$150. *Courtesy of Betty and Kenneth Hall.*

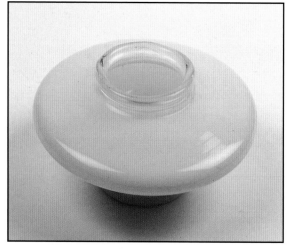

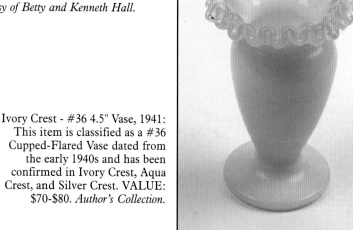

Ivory Crest - 4" Special Rose Bowl, circa 1941: A unique item that has popped up several times in Cranberry Spiral Optic and Peach Blow. No others are reported at this time in Ivory Crest. VALUE: UND. *Author's Collection.*

Ivory Crest - #36 4.5" Vase, 1941: This item is classified as a #36 Cupped-Flared Vase dated from the early 1940s and has been confirmed in Ivory Crest, Aqua Crest, and Silver Crest. VALUE: $70-$80. *Author's Collection.*

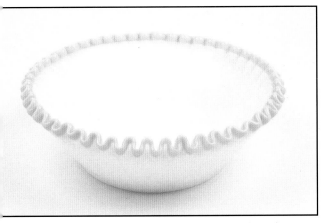

Jade Crest - 10" Salad Bowl, circa 1942. VALUE: $175-$200. *Courtesy of the Fenton Glass Museum.*

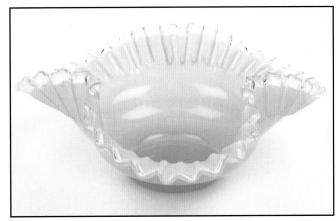

Jade Silver Crest - #152 10" Bowl, circa late 1942: Possibly made at the same time as Jade Crest and Jade Snow Crest as a sample treatment. VALUE: UND. *Courtesy of the Fenton Glass Museum.*

Peach Crest/Peach Blow - Family Punch Bowl, circa early 1940s: I use both terms here, as it is not *suppose* to be Peach Crest until it has a crystal ring put on it; but, in the case of the Aqua Creamer pictured earlier, it has no ring but a colored handle, and is considered Aqua Crest. I don't know if this way of thinking works with Peach Crest or not! This was sold to me as a Family Punch Bowl. It's possible that this was what it was used for, as it was quite common for small family gatherings in the late 1930s/early 1940s to use a bowl such as this for festive occasions! VALUE: UND. *Author's Collection.*

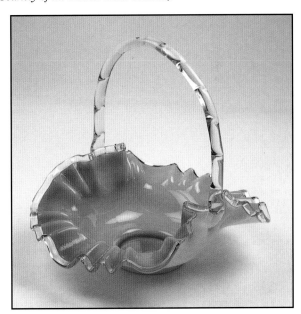

Peach Crest -Shell Crimp 10" Basket: By using the same crimp as on the large side of the #71 Shell Bowl, the worker who made this basket created a unique and different type of shape. VALUE: UND. *Author's Collection.*

Peach Crest - Looped Handled Flipped Sided 10" Basket, early 1940s: Top View.

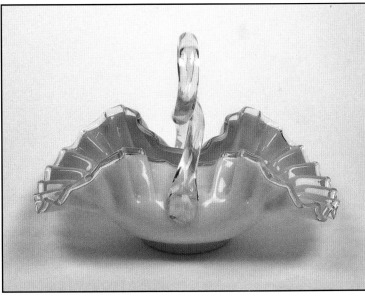

Peach Crest - Looped Handled Flipped Sided 10" Basket, early 1940s: A Whimsey that some worker must have really enjoyed making. Actually there are two of these known to exist. Coincidently, both of them are located in the same city. VALUE: UND. *Courtesy of Laurie & Richard Karman.*

57

Peach Crest – Cruet, early 1940s: This is another item where it is unclear whether it was made for Fenton's regular line or for L. G. Wright or another company. It is known that this shape has also appeared in Blue Overlay. VALUE: $200-$250. *Author's Collection.*

Peach Crest - #1523 Candlestick with Flared Straight Crimp, circa early 1940s. VALUE: UND. *Courtesy of Phil Barber.*

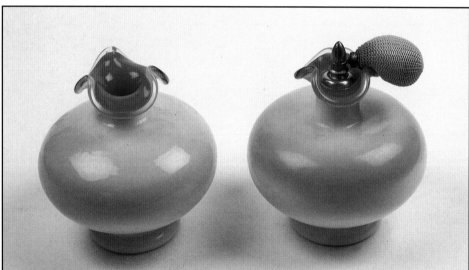

Peach Crest - DeVilBiss Atomizer/Atomizer Vase, 1940s: Fenton produced a large number of items for DeVilBiss to adapt into Atomizers and Perfumes in the 1940s, including this shape in Peach Crest, Blue Overlay, and Rose Overlay. During the same time, this shape was also sold as a vase, either by DeVilBiss or another company that Fenton produced glass for. VALUE: Atomizer: $125-$150; Vase: $80-$100. *Author's Collection.*

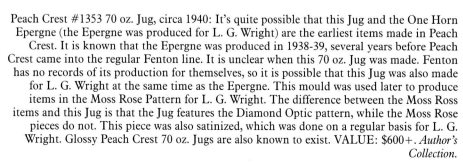

Peach Crest #1353 70 oz. Jug, circa 1940: It's quite possible that this Jug and the One Horn Epergne (the Epergne was produced for L. G. Wright) are the earliest items made in Peach Crest. It is known that the Epergne was produced in 1938-39, several years before Peach Crest came into the regular Fenton line. It is unclear when this 70 oz. Jug was made. Fenton has no records of its production for themselves, so it is possible that this Jug was also made for L. G. Wright at the same time as the Epergne. This mould was used later to produce items in the Moss Rose Pattern for L. G. Wright. The difference between the Moss Ross items and this Jug is that the Jug features the Diamond Optic pattern, while the Moss Rose pieces do not. This piece was also satinized, which was done on a regular basis for L. G. Wright. Glossy Peach Crest 70 oz. Jugs are also known to exist. VALUE: $600+. *Author's Collection.*

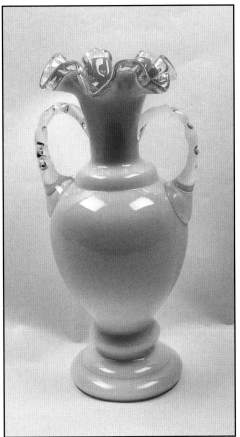

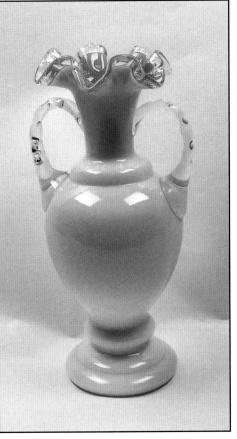

Peach Crest - #194 11" 2 Handled Vase, circa mid-1940s: Again, I don't know if these #194 items in Peach Crest were made for another company, as a special order, or if they were sampled by Fenton. A 13" 2-Handled Vase is also known to exist. VALUE: $275-$350. *Courtesy of Darcie Smith.*

Peach Crest - #194 13" 1 Handled Vase, mid-1940s: A unique and impressive item, possibly made for another individual by Fenton. VALUE: $225-$250. *Courtesy of Laurie & Richard Karman.*

Peach Crest - #194 11" Vase, mid-1940s. VALUE: $175-$200. *Author Collection.*

PEACH CREST - 13" Ewers/Spittoon, early 1940s: Three very unusual items, because of the shapes (notice the smooth edge on the ewers, as opposed to the ruffled edge pictured earlier), but also because of their histories. All three items were made for James Fenton, the brother of Frank L. and Robert Fenton. The Ewers were made for his daughter, Eva Kuhn, and the Spittoon ended up belonging to his great-granddaughter, Carolyn, by default. When Carolyn was two years old, she was in attendance at a card game that was being played by James and some other relatives. James had brought the spittoon, because he and some of the others chewed tobacco, and she decided she needed to go. As that was the only thing close, she decided to used it!! It has been in her possession since. VALUE: UND. *Courtesy of Eva Fenton Kuhn (daughter of James Fenton).*

Peach Crest - 15.5" Plate: As with most plates made by Fenton, a bowl is flared, while still hot, into the plate shape. The uniqueness of transforming this treatment into a plate comes from the fact that, as you will remember, Peach Crest is actually three layers of glass cased together. First it uses Ruby over Clear, to achieve the pink, then it is gathered over Milk Glass. When pressing this piece, all three layers are still rather hot, to say the least! It is amazing that any ever survived being made! To date, about ten of these plates have appeared on the market. VALUE: UND. *Authors Collection.*

Peach Crest 11" #192 Jug, circa 1942: A very unusual item as this is much larger than the regular 8" Jug (pictured beside it for comparison). It is not certain whether this was a sample size or a special order item made for another company. Several other items have also appeared that were produced on regular moulds but are much larger than they should be. VALUE: UND. *Courtesy of Sue Gomer.*

Peach Crest - Barcelona Ice Tea Tumbler; early 1940s: Fenton bought several Barcelona moulds from the Diamond Glass Co. in the late1930s, and used several of these moulds quite regularly at the time, including two pitcher moulds. A Cranberry Opalescent Tumbler is on display in the Fenton Museum and helps authenticate that this is indeed Fenton. VALUE: UND. *Courtesy of Eileen and Dale Robinson.*

Peach Crest - 17" #194 Lamp, circa 1940s. VALUE: (Decoration is either after market, or not fired in the lehr) UND. *Courtesy of Betty and Ike Hardman.*

Peach Crest - #3551 8" Spanish Lace Vase, circa 1960s. VALUE: UND. *Courtesy of Joan Cimini.*

Peach Crest - 7" Thumbprint Vase, circa late 1950s: Possibly produced as a sample item when Fenton was preparing to withdraw the Thumbprint pattern from the Old Virginia Glass line and pit it into their own line. VALUE: UND. *Author's Collection.*

Peach Crest - 10" Squat Vase, early 1940s: Very unusual item with an unknown mould number. VALUE: UND. *Courtesy of Betty & Ike Hardman.*

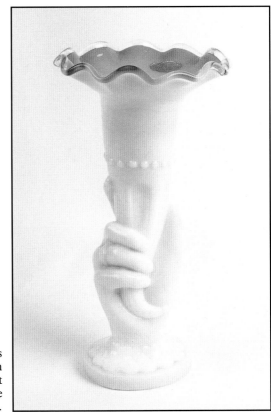

Peach Crest - #193 11.5" Hand Vase: This shape vase has had two separate issues in this treatment. The first, pictured here, was from the 1940s, and the second issue was made in 1954 at the same time that Black Rose was produced by Fenton. Although, it is somewhat hard to tell the difference between the two, the1940s issued has a smoother ruffle, while the 1954 issue has a tighter pie crust ruffle. VALUE: $300-$350. *Author's Collection.*

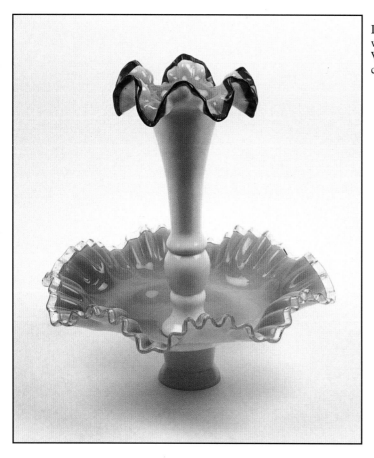

Peach Crest - L. G. Wright Epergne with Ruby Crest, circa 1942: A very unusual item, as it has a much shorter base than the regular L. G. Wright One Horn Epergne and a Ruby Crest instead of the regular clear crest. VALUE: UND. *Courtesy of Eileen and Dale Robinson.*

Crystal Peach Crest - #192 6" Jug, circa 1941: Possibly from the same time as Crystal Crest. It was decided, due to the cost of production, to go with Peach Crest. Also known is a #192 6" Vase in Crystal Peach Crest. VALUE: UND. *Courtesy of Eileen and Dale Robinson.*

Black Rose - 7" Basket; Decorated, circa 1954: Either an item that someone painted on their own or one that escaped the kiln after Abels Wasserberg had decorated it. VALUE: UND. *Courtesy of Cindy and Rick Blais.*

Black Rose - 7" Vase/#815 Cruet, circa 1954: Sample items that were tested during or prior to the time of the production of Black Rose. VALUE: UND. *Courtesy of Alice and James Rose.*

Rose Crest - Clock, circa mid-1940s: Another item that Fenton made the plate for. The plate was sold to another company who fitted a Sessions Electric Clock into the back. These clocks have also appeared in Aqua Crest, and also with "Charleton"-type flowers painted on them. VALUE: $125-$175. *Author's Collection.*

Ruby with Ruby & Milk Glass Crest/Ruby with Milk Glass Crest - #7428 8" Bonbon/#7336 8" Basket: I know that, with respect to the names employed, that this should be called Crystal Ruby Snow Crest and Ruby Snow Crest, considering the usual way that Fenton names their treatments. However, it seems that Ruby Snow Crest had already been made! Hence the "Ruby with Ruby & Milk Glass Crest" and "Ruby with Milk Glass Crest" names. Made as sample items, possibly in the 1960s. VALUE: UND. *Courtesy of Eileen and Dale Robinson.*

Ruby Crystal Crest - #187 7" Vase: When Silver Crest was first introduced, it was known as Crystal Crest, due to the extra ring of White on its edge. With this vase having that same ring of white, besides the ring of Ruby, in all probability it is called Ruby Crystal Crest. VALUE: UND. *Courtesy of Deb and Ed Volansky.*

Ruby Crest - #7336 8" Basket, circa 1960s. VALUE: UND. *Courtesy of Alice and James Rose.*

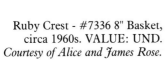

Ruby Silver Crest 10" Low Bowl or Plate, circa 1939: Made for the J. Willferd Co. in a variety of pieces. This piece has eluded most of the serious Ruby Silver Crest collectors. VALUE: UND. *Courtesy of Cindy and Rick Blais.*

Silver Crest - Spanish Lace Square Bowl, circa 1960s: A unique item, in which the Spanish Lace Cake Plate was folded up and made into a bowl. VALUE: $100-$125.

Silver Crest - Spanish Lace Square Bowl.

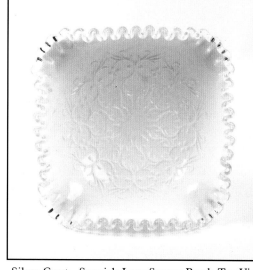

Silver Crest - Spanish Lace Square Bowl: Top View.

Silver Crest - #192 5" Rose Bowl: Possibly a sample as the regular Fenton rose bowls in the crest line were made off the #203 and #204 moulds. VALUE: UND. *Courtesy of Lynne & Gary Virden.*

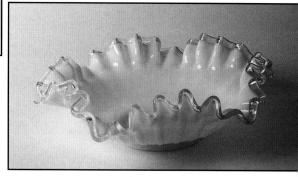

Silver Crest - 10" Ribbed Bowl, circa 1942: Made off the same blank as the Ruby Silver Crest Bowl. VALUE: UND. *Courtesy of Marylin and Dick Treiweilter.*

Silver Crest - 10" Heart-shaped Bowl, circa 1960s: This bowl, which measures approximately 10" across, is much larger than the normal heart-shaped relish pictured beside it. VALUE: UND. *Courtesy of Lynne & Gary Virden.*

Silver Crest - Tree of Life Comport: Although Fenton did do a comport in the Tree of Life Pattern in the late 1970s in Colonial Blue and Springtime Green, it was somewhat smaller than this one. Also, this comport has no logo, which puts it pre-1970s. VALUE: UND. *Courtesy of Lynne & Gary Virden.*

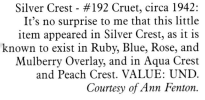

Silver Crest - #192 Cruet, circa 1942: It's no surprise to me that this little item appeared in Silver Crest, as it is known to exist in Ruby, Blue, Rose, and Mulberry Overlay, and in Aqua Crest and Peach Crest. VALUE: UND. *Courtesy of Ann Fenton.*

Silver Crest - Spanish Lace Tidbit, circa 1960s: All I have to say is never, ever be surprised at what you might run into that Fenton produced! In all the years of dealing in Fenton, I have never heard of Spanish Lace plates, much less a tidbit! VALUE: UND. *Courtesy of Laurie and Richard Karman.*

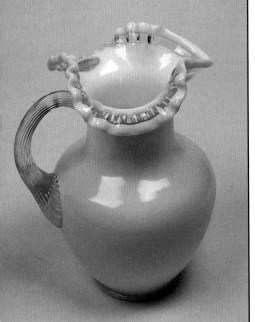

Crystal Crest - #1353 70 oz. Jug, 1942: This is a very rare item. It is surprising that it exists at all! It was in the *1950s* that the regular #1353 70 oz. Jug in Silver Crest was in Fenton catalogs. VALUE: UND. *Courtesy of Marilyn and Dick Trieweiler.*

Crystal Crest- #1353 13" Rolled Edge Console Bowl: A unique item that, surprisingly, was in Fenton's price lists in 1942. VALUE: $125-$150. *Courtesy of Marilyn and Dick Trieweiler.*

Silver Jamestown - Spittoon, circa late 1950s: Made as a Whimsey by not double crimping the ruffle. VALUE: UND. *Author's Collection.*

Silver Turquoise - Flat Comport, circa 1956: Item was sampled off the #7228 Comport to be used with a Silver Turquoise 12" Plate as a Chip 'n' Dip. VALUE: UND. *Author's Collection.*

Emerald Snow Crest - Handled 5" Vase, circa early 1950s: Made as a Whimsey by adding a small handle onto the 5" Vase. VALUE: UND. *Courtesy of Eileen and Dale Robinson.*

Blue Snow Crest - #951 Cornucopia Candlestick, circa early 1950s: Many times I stated that I would love to find a pair of Blue Snow Crest Hurricane Lamps to go along with my other Blue Snow Crest, but none have ever popped up! I will console myself with this candlestick until they do! Made in the early 1950s as a sample item. VALUE: UND. *Author's Collection.*

Amber Snow Crest - 10" 1921 Top Hat, circa early 1950s: Although in the regular Fenton line, this hat is very scarce on today's market. Shown next to the Emerald Snow Crest #170 Hurricane lamp, for a size comparison. VALUE: $150-$200. *Courtesy of Jessie and Bill Ramsey.*

Jade Snow Crest - 10" Salad Bowl, circa 1940s: Jade Snow Crest was made at the same time as Jade Crest and Crystal Jade Crest. It's unclear whether this was just a sample line, a short issued line for Fenton, or a line that Fenton produced for another company. VALUE: $175-$200.

Satin Green Silver Crest - #7221 Deep Fruit Bowl: There are no records to indicate when this item was made, but the glass resembles the Mongolian Green of the 1920s. VALUE: UND. *Courtesy of Millie Coty.*

Satin Silver Wild Rose - #1923 7" Top Hat: A beautiful item made out of Wild Rose Overlay that was satinized and then applied with a clear crest. VALUE: UND. *Courtesy of Alice and James Rose.*

Blue Crest on French Opalescent - #1477 8" Vase: A very unusual treatment, which in all probability was made after 1960 and the introduction of this mould. VALUE: UND. *Courtesy of Cindy and Rick Blais.*

Ruby Crest with Deep Blue Blown Out Interior - #1522 Bowl: Made in much the sam way as the Blown Out Peach Blow 10" Bowl (see Peach Blo in the Overlay section of this book). This piece was made t taking a bubble of blue glass and gathering it over with O and then piercing the bubble give it the blue ring in the center of the bowl. The Ruby ring was then added, making a stunning piece! VALUE: UND. *Courtesy of Phil Barber.*

Silver Crest - 10" Bowls with Amethyst, Opaque Blue, & Green Interiors, Year(s) of Production (YOP): ????: A very unusual treatments that Fenton sampled and never put into production. VALUE: UND. *Courtesy of Eileen and Dale Robinson.*

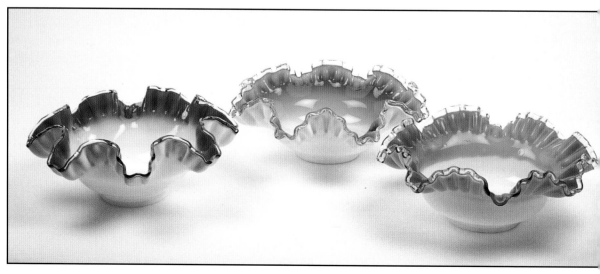

Chapter Four

Hobnail

Hobnail - Colonial Amber - #3798 Crescent Planter, circa 1960s: I listed this piece as Colonial Amber. According to Frank Fenton, it could quite possibly be a piece of Experimental Amberina. Whichever the case, it is a unique color. VALUE: UND. *Courtesy of Sharen and Al Creery.*

Hobnail - Colonial Amber - #3612 Spoon Holder, circa 1960s: The Spoon Holder in Milk Glass Hobnail Holder is rare enough that, to dream of one in another color, even if it is Amber, its completely unfathomable. It has ~~pr~~oved not to be unusual for items listed solely as ~~b~~eing made in Milk Glass to have been sampled ~~du~~ring the 1960s in the Colonial colors, and even ~~n~~ew Opalescent colors. VALUE: UND. *Courtesy of Eileen and Dale Robinson.*

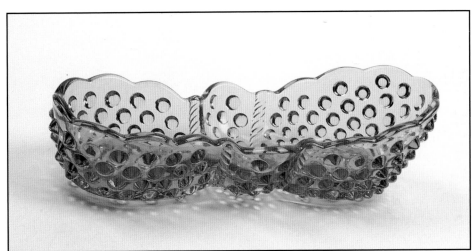

Hobnail - Black Rose - Hurricane Lamp, circa 1955: Possibly made as a sample item to see the reaction to Hobnail being produced in Black Rose. There are two variations of this lamp, one with the black crest, as shown here, and another without the crest. VALUE: UND. *Courtesy of Alice And James Rose.*

Hobnail - Blue Opalescent - Ribbon Candy Crimp 10" Basket, circa 1940s. VALUE: UND. *Courtesy of Melissia and Michael Black.*

Hobnail - Blue Opalescent - #3723 10.5" Footed Bowl, circa 1959: In 1959, Fenton reissued Topaz Opalescent; many of the pieces were only produced for 6 months. These pieces are very unusual in Topaz Opalescent, and have had a habit of popping up in both Blue and French Opalescent. That is the case with this 10.5" Footed Bowl. VALUE: $200-$250. *Courtesy of Maxine Wilson.*

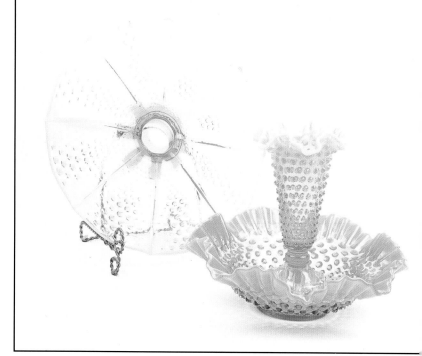

Hobnail - Blue Opalescent - 1 Horn Footed/Footed Melon Plate, circa early 1940s: In the early 1940s, at the onset of Hobnail production, there were several unusual items produced. The 1 Horn Epergne, that consisted of the 10" Bowl, Flower Frog, & Peg Vase, and the Footed Melon Plate were two of these items. Others include any other melon ribbed items in Hobnail, which were pictured in the *Fenton Glass Compendium 1940-70.* VALUE: UND. *Courtesy of the Fenton Glass Museum.*

Hobnail - Blue Opalescent - #3822 Cloverleaf Undivided Relish, 1956: I believe that this piece is just as hard to find as the same one in Milk Glass. VALUE: $300+. *Courtesy of Randy Clark Auctions.*

Hobnail - Blue Opalescent - Handled Punch Bowl, circa early 1950s: Also known to exist with a Crystal handle. Also in French Opalescent. VALUE: $1,100+. *Courtesy of Cathy and Ernie Mathus.*

Hobnail - Blue Opalescent- Handled Punch Bowl, circa early 1950s.

Hobnail - Blue Opalescent - 80 oz. Jug with Blue Plain Handle, circa 1940s: You say, "What is so unusual about this piece?" Notice the handle – most of the handles at this time were clear, with ribs, which usually appeared on the 80 oz. Jugs, or would be colored, with the Bamboo crimps. This handle is colored with no Bamboo crimps. VALUE: $300-$350. *Courtesy of Audrey and Joe Elsinger.*

Hobnail - Blue Opalescent - Decanter with Crystal Handle/Stopper, circa 1940s: It's not certain whether, in the 1940s, Fenton decided to experiment with different color combinations on their handles, as various items pop up with contrasting colors on handles from time to time. The most common occurrence of this contrast occurs when an item, such as this, appears with a colored body and a clear handle. Also featured in this picture is the regular decanter, made in 1940s and again in the 1960s, with the typical blue handle. VALUE: UND. *Courtesy of Audrey & Joe Elsinger.*

71

Hobnail - Blue Opalescent - 6" Plate on Brass Angel Stand, circa 1940s: Plate was made by Fenton and sold to another company, who fitted it with the brass stand. VALUE: $65-$75. *Courtesy of Lori and Michael Palmer.*

Hobnail - Blue Opalescent - Oil Lamp, circa 1940s: Adapted from the Mini Bud Vase, with a Burner and Chimney attached. VALUE: $150-$175. *Courtesy of Twins Antiques.*

Hobnail - Blue Opalescent - 10" Vase, circa early 1940s: Very similar to the 10" Bottle Vase, but with a little larger diameter and a wider neck and opening at the top. VALUE: UND. *Courtesy of William Lee.*

Hobnail - Blue Opalescent - Cookie Jar: When this piece first appeared in the *Big Book of Fenton*, I had no idea that such a furor it would stirred up with collectors. It has become *the* piece to own if you collect Fenton, let alone Blue Opalescent Hobnail! Made in early 1940s, it is one of the pieces that was discontinued soon after the introduction of Hobnail. VALUE: $900+. *Courtesy of Randy Clark Auctions.*

Hobnail - Blue Opalescent 6" Footed Vase, circa 1940: Very unusual crimp and ruffle. This type of ruffle is one that is not seen often. VALUE: $75-$100.

obnail - Blue/French Opalescent 5" and 6.5" Vases, circa rly 1940s: Both very similar to each other, with the Blue Vase having more of a stretch body and neck than the French Opalescent. These vases were mostly made for lamps bodies, but a good many of them have no holes rilled for the cord. VALUE: $65-$85. *Author's Collection.*

Hobnail - Blue/French/Green Opalescent - Early Wrisley Cruets, circa early 1940s: Made from the same mould as the Wrisley Cologne Bottle, these cruets are still different than the ones commonly seen in Blue, French, and Cranberry Opalescent. A regular Blue Opalescent is pictured here (second from the right). The spout is quite different from the later ones, and the neck is much narrower. In fact, I found an early Blue Opalescent cruet shortly after this picture was taken and did not realize that the neck was smaller. I tried to fit a stopper from a regular cruet into it and saw that there was at least 1/4" difference in diameter. VALUE: BLUE/ FRENCH: $150-$200; GREEN: $300+. *Courtesy of Alice and James Rose.*

Hobnail - Cranberry - Basket Whimsey: It's uncertain when this piece was made, probably in the mid-1940s. It was made off the 80 oz. jug mould. VALUE: UND. *Courtesy of Betty & Ike Hardman.*

Hobnail - Cranberry - Wrisley's Sample Bottle, 1938: In 1938, L. G. Wright approached Fenton about producing a Cranberry Hobnail Barber Bottle off of an old Northwood mould for his company. A Wrisley's representative saw this bottle and asked Fenton to design and produce one at a more modest cost in Cranberry. After one turn of these bottles was made, both Fenton and Wrisley's decided, due to production cost, that the bottle would be made in French Opalescent. It is rumored that 65 of these bottles exist. VALUE: UND. *Courtesy of Linda and John Flippen.*

Hobnail - Cranberry - 1940s Oil Bottle without Handle, circa 1941: After Wrisley's left Fenton and turned to Anchor Hocking for a cheaper bottle, Fenton retained the original moulds for the cologne bottle and used them several times over the years for other items, including the #3869 Oil Bottle. This bottle was first produced in the early 1940s for a short time in Blue, Topaz, French, and Cranberry Opalescent. It was then revamped and reissued in the 1950s in Blue, Lime, French, and Cranberry Opalescent. This bottle is unique as, for one reason or another, the handle was not applied, leaving a blank space on the bottle where is was suppose to have been. VALUE: UND. *Courtesy of Lori and Michael Palmer.*

Hobnail - Cranberry - Star Crimped Bonbon on Metal Stand, circa early 1950s: A unique item that is a fine example of an item which Fenton sold to another company, and was later fitted with the metal piece. Also know with this same stand is the standard DC Bonbon in Cranberry. VALUE: $150-$200.

Hobnail - Cranberry - Pot Belly Creamer & Sugar: Just when you think that you either have or know about all of the items in a certain pattern or color, there is one that comes along to surprise you. That was the case with this little Creamer and Sugar set. Made off of the 3" vase mould, these probably were sample items. VALUE: UND. *Courtesy of Eileen and Dale Robinson.*

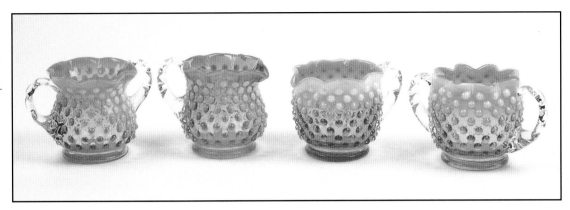

Hobnail - Cranberry - Star Crimped Creamer & Sugar/ Pot Belly Creamer & Sugar Comparison. *Courtesy of Eileen and Dale Robinson.*

Hobnail - Cranberry - Mini Creamer with Rolled Rim, circa early 1940s: Made with the same rim that was applied to the Dot Optic Creamers pictured earlier. This is the only Hobnail Creamer seen with this crimp type. VALUE: UND. *Courtesy of Trish and Harvey Holton.*

Hobnail - Cranberry - Flashed Candy Dish Lid, circa early 1950s: It's common knowledge that Cranberry Opalescent cannot be produced in pressed items; when that occurs, it becomes Plum Opalescent. When the Candy Dish was introduced in the early 1950s, it was decided, due to that fact, to produced it with either a French Opalescent lid or a Clear lid. In the case of the lid pictured here, it shows evidence that Fenton toyed with the idea of flashing the Cranberry color onto the lid, such as Westmoreland and Tiffen were doing with glass at the same time. VALUE: UND. *Courtesy of Ike & Betty Hardman.*

Hobnail - Cranberry - 4.5" Jug/Syrup Whimsey, circa early 1940s: Made off of the 4.5" Jug, this little item's opening is quite a bit smaller than the regular jug, giving it more of the appearance of a syrup pitcher. VALUE: UND. *Courtesy of Betty and Ike Hardman.*

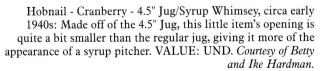

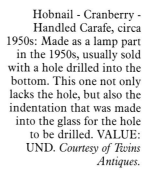

Hobnail - Cranberry - Handled Carafe, circa 1950s: Made as a lamp part in the 1950s, usually sold with a hole drilled into the bottom. This one not only lacks the hole, but also the indentation that was made into the glass for the hole to be drilled. VALUE: UND. *Courtesy of Twins Antiques.*

Hobnail - Cranberry - Mini Oil Lamps, circa 1940s: Made at the same time as the Blue Opalescent Mini Oil Lamps by adapting the Mini Bud Vase with a Burner and Chimney. VALUE: $250-$300 each. *Courtesy of Twins Antiques.*

Hobnail - Cranberry - 10" Lamps on Marble Bases made from early Oil Bottles, circa 1940s: Made from the same moulds that produced the Wrisley's bottles. These lamps were produced in the early 1940s at the same time as the early oil bottles were made. VALUE: $125-$175 each. *Courtesy of Lori and Michael Palmer.*

Hobnail - Cranberry - Mini Lamp, circa 1950s: I have seen many attempts at making the Cranberry Hobnail Candlestick into a Lamp, usually with a clear chimney attached; but never one with a complete Cranberry shade, and least of all, one with the 3" Rose Bowl made into the shade!! (Maybe that's where they are all hiding!) To say the least, a very odd item that was assembled by another company. VALUE: UND. *Courtesy of Emogene Snyder.*

Hobnail - Cranberry - 16" Lamp with Cranberry Hobnail Shade and Prisms, circa 1940s: A very ornate item, made from the Nappy, Plate, two Mini Bud Vases, and the Cranberry Chimney, that was used for a Chamber Lamp. VALUE: UND. *Courtesy of Emogene Snyder.*

Hobnail - Cranberry - Covered Jar - Cereal Bowl - Cupped Flip Vase: In any color of the Hobnail, the Covered Jar, which was only made in the early 1940s, is a true prize to find. The Cereal Bowl was made for several years, and was listed only in Milk Glass. It's unusual for it to appear in Cranberry, as it was a pressed mould. The Cupped Flip 8" Vase is another item that most advance collectors of Cranberry Hobnail are still seeking. VALUE: Covered Jar: $400+; Cereal Bowl: UND; Cupped Flipped Vase: $400+.

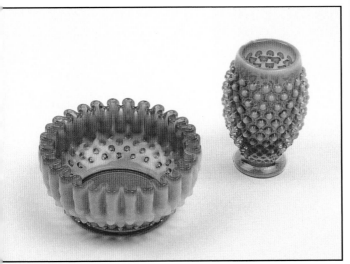

Hobnail - Cranberry - Fan Vase, Powder Jar Ashtray Whimsey: In the 1940s, the Mini Bud Vase with the Fan Top was produced. Several years later, that mould was changed to add a ruffle to the crimp, which had previously been a straight edge. (This vase is pictured on page 140 of the *Fenton Glass Compendium 1940-70.*) Later in other Opalescent colors and Milk Glass, Fenton devised the 4.5" Fan Vase. It's not certain, but highly likely, that this Fan Vase was designed as a prototype, to continue production in Cranberry, as the 4.5" Fan Vase mould was a pressed mould and could not be produced in Cranberry. The Ashtray Whimsey was made off the Powder Jar Bottom mould, possible at the same time that the DeVilBiss/Coin Dot Ashtray was produced. VALUE: UND. *Courtesy of John and Linda Flippen.*

Hobnail - Cranberry - Cereal Bowl/Cupped in Mini Bud Vase: Another view of the Cereal Bowl in Cranberry. As for the Mini Bud Vase, many people took noticed when the Green Opalescent and Blue Opalescent, first appeared in the *Big Book of Fenton 1940-70.* This type of crimp must not have been produced for long, as few seldom appear now. VALUE: UND. *Courtesy of Alice and James Rose.*

Hobnail - Cranberry - #3752 Whimsey Vases: It's not often that two similar Whimsey items appear off the same mould, even more unlikely that the same person is luckily enough to own them. These two vases were produced off the #3752 11" Vase, produced from 1967-78. As both are unmarked, it is safe to assume they were produced prior to 1970. VALUE: UND. *Courtesy of Mary Knight.*

Hobnail - Cranberry - 8" Pie Crust Crimp Vase, 1940s. VALUE: $225-$275. *Courtesy of Linda and John Flippen.*

Hobnail - Cranberry - 8" Straight Edge Vase, circa 1941-42: Another item produced with the uncommon straight edge ruffle. VALUE: UND. *Courtesy of Linda and John Flippen.*

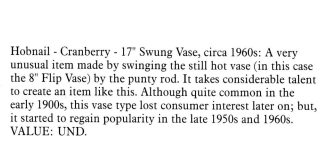

Hobnail - Cranberry - 17" Swung Vase, circa 1960s: A very unusual item made by swinging the still hot vase (in this case the 8" Flip Vase) by the punty rod. It takes considerable talent to create an item like this. Although quite common in the early 1900s, this vase type lost consumer interest later on; but, it started to regain popularity in the late 1950s and 1960s. VALUE: UND.

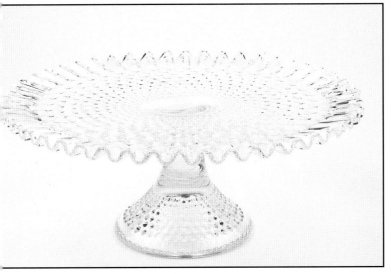

Hobnail - Crystal - Footed Cake Plate, circa early 1940s: Crystal Hobnail was issued for a brief time in the early 1940s. Also, during the war, when bone ash could not be obtain for the Opalescent, it is probable that Crystal Hobnail was made in place of French Opalescent Hobnail. Finally, a limited number of items have appeared from moulds, dating from the 1960s. In all cases, though not collected by many people, these items are very scarce. VALUE: $100-$125.

Hobnail - Crystal - Dresser Set/Mini Bud Vase, circa early1940s: Other items that were produced when bone ash could not be obtained for the production of French Opalescent. VALUE: Dresser Set: $150-$200; bud vase: $25-$35.

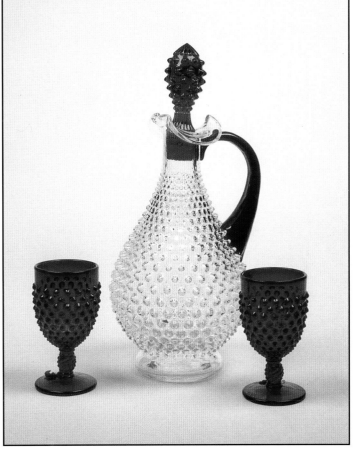

Hobnail - Crystal - Decanter with Red Handle: It's very hard to determined when this item was produced, as the Decanter mould was in used three times during the past 60 + years. The mould was first used in the 1940s, in the original issue of Hobnail Opalescent; then in 1959-61; and then it was made only in Ruby in the mid-1970s. At any time, some of these could of been produced in Crystal, with a Ruby Handle; but, it was more likely during the first or third runs of this item, as Ruby was one of the colors that Fenton was using at both times. VALUE: UND. *Courtesy of Audrey and Joe Elsinger.*

Hobnail - Crystal - 5" Vase/5" Rose Bowl. VALUE: $55-$65 each. *Courtesy of Diane and Tom Rohow.*

Hobnail - French Opalescent - 8.5" Bowls, circa 1970s: Made off the same mould as the #3638 Baskets, these bowls were never in the regular Fenton line. They were possibly made and sold at the Gift Shop in the 1970s. VALUE: UND. *Courtesy of Melva and Rick McGinnis.*

Hobnail - "Dope" Opalescent - Mini Bud Vase: Where the term "Dope" Opalescent came from I do not know, but I have been told this is the term used to refer to this color. To me, it looks as if it is a dirty brown Plum Opalescent. That could be the case, as quite a bit of experimenting was done in an attempt to make Cranberry Opalescent. This could have been one of the items produced during one of those attempts. VALUE: UND. *Courtesy of Eileen and Dale Robinson.*

Hobnail - French Opalescent - Peg Vase, circa early 1940s. VALUE: UND.

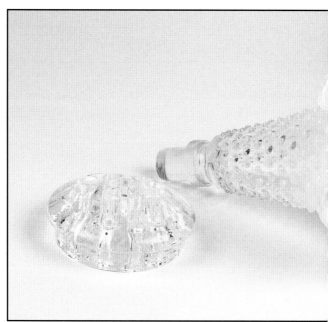

Hobnail - French Opalescent - Peg Vase, circa early 1940s: Close-up.

Hobnail - French Opalescent - Tower Candy Jar: Some of the fun of doing these books comes from playing with the glass . . . and *sometimes* with peoples minds. Admittedly, this item is a put together piece. Using the #3880 Candy jar and an extra bottom, this piece answers the question, "What do you do when you break a lid to one of the candies?" *Courtesy of Melva and Rick McGinnis.*

Hobnail - French Opalescent - Cocktail Goblet: There is no indication at the Fenton Factory when, or in what other colors, these little Goblets were produced. VALUE: UND. *Courtesy of Melva and Rick McGinnis.*

Hobnail - French Opalescent - Offset Lamp made from a Handled Candlestick, circa 1950s: Made from the mould that was originally marketed in Cranberry and Milk Glass. Few of these have surfaced in French Opalescent. It might have been that most of the ones produced in this color ended up as lamps!! VALUE: UND. *Courtesy of Lori and Michael Palmer.*

Hobnail - French Opalescent - Lamp Fashioned from Cookie Jar, circa 1940s: I had mentioned earlier that it was possible that virtually anything that Fenton made could also have been produced as a lamp. This is a prime example! Notice the matching metal cover and foot. This proves that the piece wasn't a home made job. VALUE: $250-$300. *Courtesy of Melva and Rick McGinnis.*

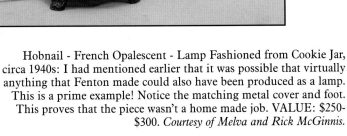

Hobnail - French Opalescent - Lamp, circa 1940s: Although this lamp was made up, in part, with one regular Fenton lamp part (the 7" Special Rose Bowl), the bottom of a Wrisley's Ginger Jar was also used. It is very odd for a piece that Fenton produced for another company to end mixed together with yet another firm's glass in a lamp! VALUE: $200-$300. *Courtesy of Melva and Rick McGinnis.*

Hobnail - French Opalescent - Lamp. VALUE: $150-$200. *Courtesy of Melva and Rick McGinnis.*

Hobnail - French Opalescent – Bottles: Both bottles were shown in my earlier book *The Big Book of Fenton Glass 1940-70* in Blue Opalescent. As I stated in that book, both shapes were used for lamp parts and also sold as vases. VALUE: $55-$65 each. *Courtesy of Melva and Rick McGinnis.*

Hobnail - French Opalescent – Cupped-in Ruffled Mini Bud Vase: This is the only time that I have ever see a Mini Bud Vase with the Rose Bowl Cupped-in Crimp. Imagine the excitement that a Cranberry example in this color would cause! VALUE: UND. *Courtesy of Alice and James Rose.*

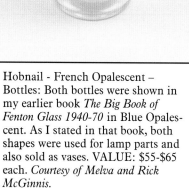

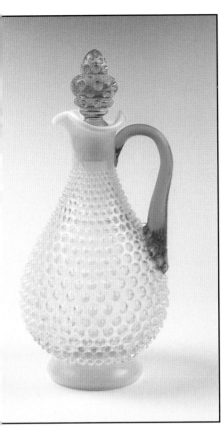

Hobnail - Deep Green Opalescent - Squat Jug: Much darker than the regular Green Opalescent Hobnail from the 1940s, but still lighter than the Deep Green Opalescent (Emerald Green or Blue-Green) Opalescent from the late 1950s. It still is a mystery as to when this piece was produced. VALUE: UND. *Courtesy of Betty & Ike Hardman.*

Hobnail - French Opalescent - Decanter with Blue Handle, circa 1940s: As I stated earlier, it was not unusual for Fenton to produced items, from time to time, with a body in one color and a contrasting handle color. This is one classic example. It makes you wonder if they were not inspired by this piece, years later, when they came up with their French Opalescent decorated items with colored Crests. VALUE: UND. *Courtesy of Betty and Ike Hardman.*

Hobnail - Green Opalescent - Dresser Set in Metal Holder, 1940: At least, due to the short production run for this color in Hobnail, we can date this set to the early part of 1940. This set was sold to another company and was then fitted with the brass holders. VALUE: UND. *Courtesy of Janice and Gordy Bowerman.*

Hobnail - Green Opalescent - Low Candle Holder/Comport: Another pair of items that are a puzzle as to when they were made. Green Opalescent in Hobnail had been discontinued for almost a year before these candlesticks came into the line, and for twenty years before this comport was introduced. Some will say that this is a light Deep Green Opalescent (Emerald or Blue Green) from the 1960s; but, these items do not have the right color base to match Deep Green Opalescent. VALUE: Candlesticks: $40-$50 each; Comport: $80-$100. *Courtesy of Betty and Ike Hardman.*

Hobnail - Green Opalescent - Covered Jar - Tall Covered Jar; 1940: Any serious Hobnail collector is aware of this elusive Covered Jar, produced in Cranberry, Blue, Topaz, French, and Green Opalescent from 1940 to circa 1943. Not many are aware of what is referred to as the "Tall Jar." Very rare, and seldom seen, this jar is know for sure in Blue Opalescent, but none have come to light as yet in Cranberry, French, or Topaz Opalescent. Also, for another shape of Jar that has appeared only in Cranberry, see page 101 in the *Fenton Glass Compendium*. VALUE: Short Covered Jar: $400-$500; Tall Covered Jar: UND.

Hobnail - Green Opalescent - Mini Bottle. VALUE: UND. *Courtesy of Tina and Joe Boris.*

Hobnail - Green Opalescent - 8.5" Jug, 1940: Made from the Tankard Jug mould, this jug very much resembles the 5.5" Jug that was a regular in the Hobnail line at that time. VALUE: UND. *Author's Collection.*

Hobnail - Green Opalescent/Topaz Opalescent - 7.5" Bonbons. VALUE: UND. *Courtesy of Thomas K. Smith.*

Hobnail - Green Opalescent - 6.25" Fan Vase: This item (and several others) has appeared, from time to time, over the years much paler and more washed out in color than the regular Green Opalescent. Sometime it is referred to as Telephone Insulator Green Opalescent. VALUE: $80-$100. *Author's Collection.*

Hobnail - Green Overlay - Vanity Lamps, circa late 1940s: Made by Fenton for another company, who again bought the glass parts and fashioned them into a lamp. This shape is know in Blue Opalescent, French Opalescent, and Topaz Opalescent, but has never been documented before in Green Overlay. VALUE: UND. *Author's Collection.*

Hobnail - Kitchen Green - 80 oz. Jug: I know the Jadeite lovers are just dying over this! Kitchen Green is the color name that Fenton gave its Jade, when used for Kitchenware, such as the Mixing Bowls made for Doromeyer in the 1930s. This color had pretty much been discontinued by the time that Hobnail came into existence, except for the Doromeyer bowls. This was a sample item, so there is no telling how many of these were produced, or what else in Hobnail might be out there. VALUE: UND. *Courtesy of Eileen and Dale Robinson.*

Hobnail - Lime Opalescent - Bonbon on Stand/Bonbon Candlestick: Two other items for which the glass parts were produced by Fenton and sold to another company, where they added other pieces. VALUE: Bonbon on Stand: $90-$110; Bonbon Candlestick: $90-$110.

Hobnail - Lime Opalescent/Lime Opalescent Satin – Cruet 1953: Although in Fenton's regular line, the Lime Opalescent Hobnail Cruet is a decided rarity, made only for one year in this very briefly issued color. The Lime Opalescent Satin Hobnail Cruet is even more of a rarity, as very few items made by Fenton were satinized at this time. VALUE Lime Opalescent: $300+; Lime Opalescent Satin: UND.

Hobnail – Mandarin Red - Mini B Vase: Manderian Red had been discontinued for good while before the introduction Hobnail, so it's very uncommon see a piece of it to pop up in this color. VALUE: UND. *Courtesy of Eileen and Dale Robinson.*

Hobnail - Mulberry Overlay - Gone With The Wind Lamp: "Unique" or "rare" are the least that can be said about this lamp! Made as a sample item when Fenton first decided to bring back the Mulberry color in the early 1980s. When the present owners bought this item, by mail order, as Plum Opalescent, they were disappointed when it did not have any Opal in it. When they asked Frank Fenton about this piece, he told them not to be disappointed, it was much better than Plum! There are times when misrepresentation is a *good* thing! VALUE: UND. *Courtesy of Carolyn and Dick Grable.*

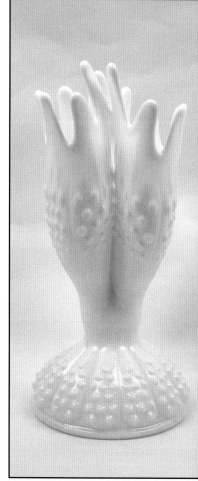

Hobnail - Milk Glass – Vase, made from the #3745 Candle Holder, circa 1960s: Another glassworker gone mad! With this piece, they actually took the Candleholder, while still warm, and pushed it down into itself to make a vase. VALUE: UND. *Courtesy of Shirley Masters.*

Hobnail - Opal - Fairy Lamp/Boudoir Lamp, 1960s: Very similar to Milk Glass, but, according to Fenton catalogs, this glass was more heat resistance and had better translucent properties than Milk Glass. VALUE: Fairy Lamp: $30-$40; Boudoir Lamp: UND. *Courtesy of Wanell and Walt Jones.*

Hobnail - Colonial Orange Satin/Flame Crest Hobnail? 12 oz. Syrup Jugs, circa mid-1960s: Two unique items, as the 12 oz. Syrup was never produced in regular Colonial Orange to begin with. So this was obviously a sample item. The Flame Crest Syrup Jug could be consider either way, either as a Whimsey made by a handler who slipped a Colonial Orange handle onto a Milk Glass Jug or as a sample item at the time that Flame Crest was in production. VALUE: UND.

Hobnail - Pastel Milk Glass - Blue Pastel - #3822 Undivided Relish, 1954: Many times I have joked about the same shape, in White Milk Glass, and how if you listed one on Ebay, the phone lines would possibly melt down! Little did I realize that such a rare and unusual item would exist in this color! My day was completely made when I found this piece, along with about six other items that are featured in this book! VALUE: UND. *Author's Collection.*

Hobnail - Orange Opalescent - 11" Vase/10" Bowl: Again, a very rare color that was sampled in the mid-1960s. With this 11" Vase shape appearing in Cranberry in 1967, it would be safe to assume that Orange Opalescent was sampled close to that time. VALUE: UND.

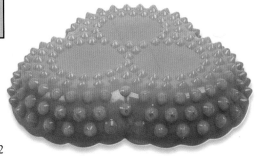

Hobnail - Pastel Milk Glass - Blue Pastel - #3822 Undivided Relish, 1954: Back side of Relish.

Hobnail - Pastel Milk Glass - Turquoise - Sherbets/Water Goblet: There is no record of these items being produced in this color at the Fenton Factory. It was possibly a sample run. I personally have seen no other Sherbets and only one other Water Goblet. VALUE: UND.

Hobnail - Pastel Milk Glass-Rose Pastel/Green Pastel - 5" Vase/Jardinière, circa mid-1950s: The Rose Pastel 5" Vase probably was sampled in 1955 or 1956, at the same time that Turquoise Hobnail was in production, as the 5" vase was in regular production in that color and it was not unusual for Fenton to used the same shapes in similar colors. The Jardinière, according to Frank Fenton, was made for A. L. Randall's of Chicago, for their Florist catalogs. It was in production for several years, but is seldom seen on the market today. VALUE: UND. *Author's Collection.*

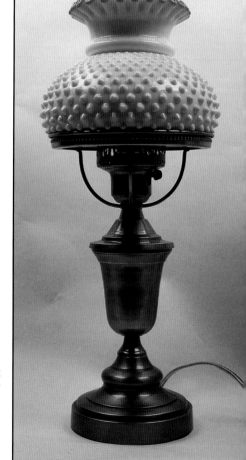

Hobnail - Peach Blow - 16" Student Lamp. VALUE: $250-$300. *Courtesy of Darice Smith.*

Hobnail - Plum Opalescent - 14" Plate, circa 1983: Made off the 12" Bowl that Fenton produced in the early 1980s for Levay of Edwardsville, Illinois. VALUE: UND. *Courtesy of Carolyn and Dick Grable.*

Hobnail - Purple/Grape Opalescent - 5" Vase: Much darker and denser than Plum Opalescent, this item also has the Fenton logo on the bottom, with no decade mark, which would date its production prior to 1980. Keep in mind, that Fenton reissued Plum Opalescent Hobnail in the early 1980s for Levay of Edwardsville, Illinois, and this could have been sampled shortly before that time. The owner of this piece prefers to call this color Grape Opalescent. VALUE: UND.

Hobnail - Rose Overlay - Decanter, circa 1942: Produced sometime during the short run of Rose Overlay Hobnail, but not listed on any of the price sheets or in the Fenton catalog at the time. It was somewhat amusing to me, when I mentioned this piece to Frank Fenton several years ago, when he made the statement that it didn't exist and I had to tell him that I had just taken this picture of it. VALUE: UND. *Courtesy of Betty and Ike Hardman.*

Hobnail - Ruby Cased Milk Glass – Decanter: Probably made in the late 1970s, when Fenton had the decanter produced in Ruby Hobnail. VALUE: UND. *Courtesy of Ike and Betty Hardman.*

Hobnail - Ruby Carnival - Decanter, circa 1970s: Sampled at the same time that the regular Ruby Hobnail was in the line. VALUE: UND. *Courtesy of Audrey and Joe Elsinger.*

Hobnail - Satin Crystal - Mini Bud Vase: Made during the run of regular crystal Hobnail prior to WWII, or during the war, when bone ash could no be obtained for the Opalescent. For some reason this item ended up satinized. VALUE: UND. *Courtesy of Andrew and Randi Jenkins.*

Hobnail - Topaz Opalescent - Cereal Bowl: Possibly made at the same time as the Cranberry Cereal Bowl pictured earlier. It sometimes makes your wonder, with items such as this popping up, what other items were made off of Milk Glass moulds in color! VALUE: UND.

Hobnail - Topaz Opalescent - 12" Oval Bowl: Made in the late 1950s or early 1960s at a time when Fenton was sampling many of their Milk Glass moulds in various colors. VALUE: UND. *Courtesy of Susie, Tiffany, and Ron Ballard.*

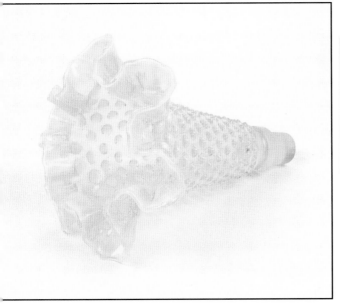

Hobnail - Topaz Opalescent - Peg Vase, early 1940s: With the appearance of the French Opalescent Peg Vase, after the Blue Opalescent example had been pictured in the *Big Book of Fenton 1940-70*, it is not really surprising to me that a Topaz vase has surfaced. Now, I'm waiting for my Green Opalescent vase to come out of the woodwork! VALUE: UND. *Courtesy of William Lee.*

Hobnail - Topaz Opalescent - Cookie Jar, circa early 1940s: Although several of the Blue and French Opalescent Jars have surfaced over the past several years, which leads me to believe that they were in the regular line, only around three of the Topaz Jars have surfaced. This indicates to me that, although they were listed in the 1942 price lists, they are much harder to find. VALUE: $1,500+. *Courtesy of William Lee.*

Hobnail - Topaz Opalescent - Large Bottle, early 1940s: Made off the same mould as the Wrisley's Cruet Bottles, this one came out minus the handle. The neck and opening is somewhat larger and does take the regular cruet stopper. VALUE: UND. *Courtesy of William Lee.*

Hobnail - Topaz Opalescent - Large Bottle/Cupped Flipped Vase/Footed 6" Vase, circa early 1940s. VALUE: Large Bottle: UND; Cupped Flipped Vase: $400+; Footed 6" Vase: 100-$125.

Hobnail - Topaz Opalescent - DeVilBiss Atomizer, early 1940s: Made for the DeVilBiss Company in the early 1940s. You see a good number of Blue and French Opalescent Hobnail Atomizers, but seldom a Topaz one. VALUE: $150-$200.

Hobnail - Topaz Opalescent - Sherbets: Possibly sampled in the mid-1950s, before Topaz Opalescent was reintroduced into the Hobnail Line. There are two complete sets of eight known in these sherbets. VALUE: UND. *Courtesy of Wanell and Walt Jones.*

Hobnail - Topaz Opalescent - 80 oz. Ice Lip Jug/Water Goblet/Footed Ice Tea: The Pitcher was possibly produced in the 1940s as a Whimsey item. A Pitcher in Blue Opalescent with the same ice lip is know to exist. The Goblet and Footed Ice Tea again, was possibly produced in the mid-1950s, to sample Topaz Opalescent VALUE: UND. *Courtesy of William Lee.*

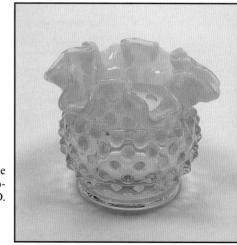

Hobnail - Topaz Opalescent - 3" Vase: Another item from the late 1950s that was used to sample this color before it's reintroduction to the Hobnail line. VALUE: UND.

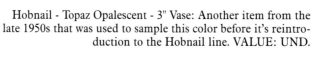

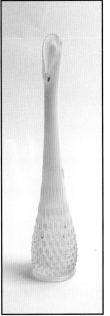

Hobnail - Topaz Opalescent - Flat Bud Vase: Very unusual item, possibly a Whimsey. VALUE: UND. *Courtesy of Kill Creek Antique.*

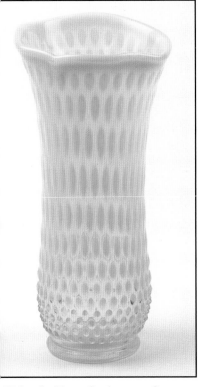

Hobnail - Topaz Opalescent - Swung Vase, circa 1959: A variation of the Regular Large Swung Vase. VALUE: UND. *Courtesy of Ike and Betty Hardman.*

Hobnail - Topaz Opalescent - 8" Flip Vases: Very few of these surface, although they were in the regular line of Hobnail items throughout the first run of Topaz Opalescent. The one on the left is referred to as the Cupped Flared, and the one on the right is the Cupped-in. VALUE: $300+ each. *Courtesy of William Lee.*

Hobnail - Wild Rose - Covered Jar: Produced possibly in the 1940s, at the same time of Rose Overlay, maybe as a sample color. This color is somewhat lighter than the regular Wild Rose Overlay produced in the early 1960s. VALUE: UND. *Author's Collection.*

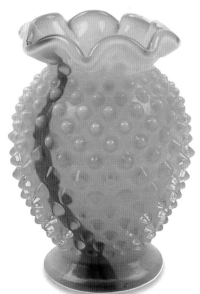

Hobnail - Yellow Overlay Opalescent Swirl - Mini Bud Vase: The name of this color is a mouth full. Very unusual item, especially with the dark brown stripe running through it, giving it a slag effect. VALUE: UND. *Courtesy of Betty and Ike Hardman.*

Hobnail - Wild Rose - Lamp Base Fount: Probably made at the same time as the Wild Rose Jar, either for another company to adapt into a lamp, or to use to sample color. VALUE: UND. *Courtesy of Maxine Wilson.*

93

Chapter Five
Opalescent

Opalescent - Wisteria Opalescent - Diamond Optic - #192A Cologne Bottle, circa 1942: Made about the same time as the Wisteria Opalescent Hobnail for the Sherwin Williams Paint Company. No records of this item in this color exist. Possibly it was a sample. VALUE: UND. *Author's Collection.*

Opalescent - Blue - Glossy Swirled Feather - #815 Large Cologne, circa 1953: First I want to clarify the term Glossy when used by Fenton. Throughout Fenton's history, in lines that were *only* issued in Satin glass, where an item for one reason or another would escape the satinizing process, that item would be classified as Glossy. The Swirl Feather line is one such case, where a "satin-free" item would be called Glossy Swirl Feather. These items, especially in the Swirled Feather line, are highly prized by advanced Fenton collectors. In the same vein, at one time I made the comment that later on in the 1970s, when Fenton produced the Blue Satin and Lime Satin line (where Satin was in the name of the line), when an item appeared in that line, it was glossy and would be called "Glossy Blue Satin" or "Glossy Lime Satin." I was quickly told by several that the term just wouldn't work! Now, as many of you can tell, this cologne bottle in Glossy Blue Swirled Feather is much larger than the regular cologne bottle, as it was made from the #815 Cruet mould. VALUE: UND. *Courtesy of Janice and Gordy Bowerman.*

Opalescent - Blue - Butterfly Net - #1942 Goblet, 1942: Made by Fenton for another company, either as a sample or an extremely short issue. Eight items are know to exist in this pattern, including the Goblet, Sherbet, Cocktail, Wine, 12 oz. Tumbler, Finger Bowl, 6" Plate, 8" Plate, and 4" Cup Plate. Also known in French Opalescent in these pieces. This mould was originally made in 1938 for the Historic American line, which Macy's Department Stores of New York had Fenton produced for them. The moulds were later retooled into the Butterfly Net pattern. The pattern was named by William Heacock in honor of the Fenton Art Glass Collectors Club of America. VALUE: UND.

Opalescent - Blue Satin - Swirled Feather – Atomizer, 1953. VALUE: $350-$400. *Courtesy of Linda and John Flippen.*

palescent - Cranberry/Lime Green - Glossy Swirled Feather - 2005 Cologne Bottles, 1953: Again, these two escaped the tinizing process. You might keep in mind, also, that some items at is time, that were meant to be produced in Satin, have the optic in palescent, but still have an opaque look to the glass (*see* the Glossy reen 7" Rib Optic Vase and Glossy Rose Rib Optic Cruet in this hapter). VALUE: Cranberry: $400-$475; Green Opal: $500-$575. *ourtesy of Ike and Betty Hardman.*

Opalescent - French Satin - Swirled Feather – Atomizer, 1953: Most people are aware of the three main colors in Swirled Feather, which are Rose Satin, Green Satin, and Blue Satin. All three of these colors are almost impossible to find. Many collectors don't realize that Swirled Feather was also done in French Satin (French Opalescent Satinized for the uninformed!). Seldom does any Swirled Feather ever appears in this color, so it's surprising when this bottle popped up, especially fitted with an atomizer bulb. VALUE: $300-$350.

Opalescent - Rose Satin - Swirled Feather - #2005 Cologne Bottle/ Powder Jar, 1953: What is so different about these items, you ask? As for the powder jar . . . nothing, it is there for pictorial purposes. However, notice the cologne, which is fitted with an adaptor that takes the screw-in stopper laying in front of it. This is another item that was made by Fenton and sold to another company, either DeVilBiss or someone else who fitted it with the adaptor. You might note that this adaptor was the same one used to fit the Atomizer Bulbs into the cologne bottles at this time. VALUE: UND. *Courtesy of Janice and Gordy Bowerman.*

Opalescent - French Opalescent/Cranberry Opalescent - Fairy Light/
Cologne Bottle. VALUE: Bottle: $350-$500; Fairy Light: $650-$750.

Opalescent - Lime Green - Glossy Swirled Feather - #2098 Hurricane Lamp, 1953. VALUE: UND. *Courtesy of Audrey and Joe
Elsinger.*

Opalescent - French Satin - Swirled Feather - 10" Vase: For over
thirty years, it was a stated fact that there were just six different
items in Swirled Feather. Now this piece shows up and bursts that
theory to pieces. Made off the #183 mould, possibly as a sample
item. VALUE: UND. *Courtesy of Williamstown Antique Mall.*

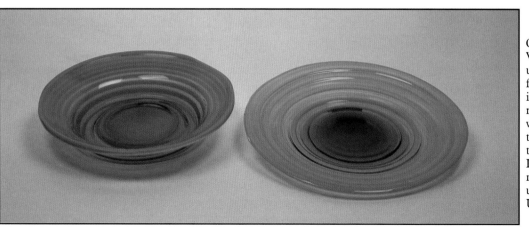

Opalescent - Green Opalescent - Ne
World - 9" Plate/Cereal Bowl, 1953:
unique case in which the plate, whe
first formed, is not flatten out, but l
in a bowl shape. Many people do n
realize that, when making plates in
way that they are produced at Fent
they are made into bowl shapes firs
then flattened and formed into pla
In this case, the bowl this size was
never marketed, making it much m
unusual than the plate. VALUE:
UND.

Opalescent - Cased Black/Grey - New World - #7347 Wine Goblets, 1953: A unique item in a very rare color. So rare, and off beat, it would be hard to say how many people would pass by them in a shop or an antique show, not realizing that they are Fenton. VALUE: $140-$150. *Courtesy Carolyn and Dick Grable.*

Opalescent - Blue Opalescent - New World - #1667 Wine Bottle, 1950s: Always keep in mind that New World was only made in Opalescent, in Lime, and Cranberry. So, when you see a piece like this one in another color, you don't want to pass it by! VALUE: UND. *Courtesy of Eileen and Dale Robinson.*

Opalescent - Lime Opalescent - Topaz Opalescent - Cranberry - New World -#1667/1747 Wine Bottles/Goblets, 1950s: Although the Lime and Cranberry Bottles and Goblets were in the regular New World line, the Topaz Bottle was made much later, possibly around 1959, when Topaz Opalescent was reintroduced in the Fenton line. Keep in mind that, although most pieces and colors of New World were discontinued in 1954, the Wine Bottle in Cranberry was in the line until the early 1960s. VALUE: TOPAZ OPAL: UND; CRANBERRY: $175-$200; LIME: $275-$300.

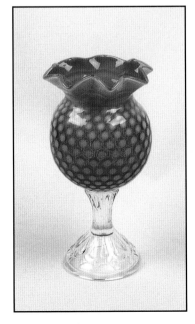

Opalescent - Cranberry - Polka Dot - Ruffled Ivy Ball, 1956: Made as a Whimsey item, as the regular Ivy Ball had a straight edge. VALUE: UND. *Courtesy of Emogene Snyder.*

Opalescent - Cranberry - Polka Dot - Ivy Ball Oil Lamp, 1956: Many years ago, when I first saw this shape of Ivy Ball, I actually thought it was the base for an Oil Lamp! It goes to show that maybe I'm not as off beat as many think I am! This piece was purchased from Fenton by another company and then adapted with the burner. VALUE: UND. *Courtesy of Emogene Snyder.*

Opalescent - Cranberry - Polka Dot - Sugar Shaker, 1956: It's quite unusual for a line such as Polka Dot to have any Samples or Whimseys, as it was only made for six months. But here is one of its mysteries. The Sugar Shaker on the right was the one that was in the regular Polka Dot line. The one on the left looks like the Polka Dot pattern, only it's on an L. G. Wright Sugar Shaker mould. It could of been that, when Fenton was developing the Polka Dot pattern, they borrowed some moulds off of L. G. Wright to test out shapes with the pattern, as they never had a sugar shaker in their own line before. VALUE: UND. *Courtesy of Eileen and Dale Robinson.*

Opalescent - French Opalescent - Fine Dot - #1922 9" Top Hat: Items in this pattern appeared in the 1938 catalog in Crystal, listed as an "Unusual Crystal Assortment." Later, some of these items appeared in Ruby Overlay in the 1940s and 1950s. Even later, a few of these moulds were adapted for use in Fenton's Ruby Overlay issued of the 1950s, which many people refer to as "Thumbprint." It was during this time, probably in the late 1930s or early 1940s, that this hat was produced in French Opalescent, maybe in 1938 when Fenton was beginning Opalescent production. Many items appeared that year in both Cranberry and French Opalescent. VALUE: $150-$200. *Courtesy of Betty and Ike Hardman.*

Opalescent - Cranberry - Polka Dot - Sugar Shaker Vase, 1956: The late Ruth Grizel, author of several books on Westmoreland and of the *American Slag Glass* book, once commented to me, on the subject of Whimseys, that the "Workers would get funny after hours." That had to be the case with this vase. Not only was it adapted from a sugar shaker, but the enterprising worker also pulled down the edge into a unique rolled rim. VALUE: UND. *Courtesy of Eileen and Dale Robinson.*

Opalescent - Topaz Opalescent - Spiral Optic - #1353 Ice Lipped Jug/#1925 6" Vase/#1923 7" Basket, 1938: I stated earlier in this book that in Dot Optic the rarest color is Topaz Opalescent. This also holds true in Spiral Optic. It's very seldom that any items in Topaz Spiral Optic appear on the market, so it is a real treasure when you have a grouping such as this in a collection. VALUE: Jug: $500-$600; #1925 6" Vase: $200-$250; #1923 7" Basket: $200-$250.

Opalescent - Cranberry - Spiral Optic - Bottle Vase, 1938: Made off the same mould as the previously pictured Dot Optic Vase (in this book in Blue Opalescent and in the *Fenton Glass Compendium 1940-70* in French Opalescent). It might be noted that a piece in this shape has also appeared drilled and made into a lamp. VALUE: UND. *Courtesy of Linda and John Flippen.*

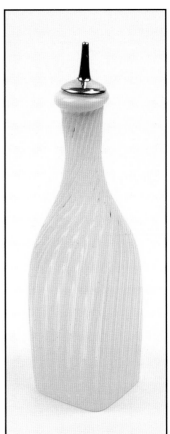

Opalescent - Topaz Opalescent - Spiral Optic - Square Barber Bottle, circa late 1930s. This bottle was sampled by Fenton but never put into the regular line, a very rare and unique item! VALUE: UND. *Courtesy of Alice and James Rose.*

Opalescent - Blue Opalescent - Spiral Optic - Unusual Rose Bowl, circa 1939: Unique item, I'm not sure if it was meant as a Rose Bowl, Vase, or maybe a bottle for a jar. VALUE: UND. *Author's Collection.*

Opalescent - Cranberry - Spiral Optic - 4" Special Rose Bowl, 1938-39: Not only is the 4" Rose Bowl a rarity in itself, but notice the opening, which is much larger than the regular special rose bowls. VALUE: $100-$150. *Courtesy of Linda and John Flippen.*

Opalescent - Cranberry - Spiral Optic - 8.5" Bowl: It's hard to say when this item was made by Fenton, and whether it was made for them or they made it for L. G. Wright, as this was also a regular shape for an L. G. Wright lamp shade. I have seen this shape in different patterns in both Fenton and L. G. Wright, made into lamp shades and also, with the bottom still intact, as a bowl. VALUE: UND. *Courtesy of Emogene Snyder.*

Opalescent - Cranberry - Spiral Optic 8.5" Bowl: Another of what could be referred to as "Lamp Shade Bowls" in Spiral Optic. Notice the difference in crimps. VALUE: UND.

Opalescent - Cranberry - Spiral Optic - 10" Bowl in Brides Bowl Frame, late 1930s: Normally I would say that someone "Married" these two pieces together; but, over the past 5 or 6 years I have seen several of these in this exact holder! On looking closer, you can tell that the silver fittings fit the ruffles exactly. So, it's too much of a coincidence to consider that it wasn't sold that way. Again, it was a case of another company buying the bowl and fitting the brass holder onto it. Keep in mind that several importers, over the past 30 years, have made a big business out of doing the exact same thing with bowls that look similar to Fenton's. VALUE: $250-$300. *Courtesy of Linda and John Flippen.*

Opalescent - Cranberry - Spiral Optic - #192 5" Squat Vase/#1924 Creamer/#203 7" Bowl, 1938-39: Three very hard to find items in Spiral Optic. The creamer is one that most advance collectors of Fenton Spiral Optic do not have in their collections. VALUE: #192 Vase: $150-$175; #1924 Creamer: $175-$200; #203 7" Bowl: $100-$125. *Courtesy Linda and John Flippen.*

Opalescent - Cranberry - Spiral Optic - #1920 12" Top Hat/#1921 11" Top Hat/#1924 4" Top Hat: It's very seldom that one sees the two large sizes of these hats in a collection of glass. Two of these sizes of top hats made by Fenton include the #1923 7" Top Hat and the #1922 9" Top Hat. VALUE: #1920 12": UND; #1921 11": $400-$500; #1924 4": $100-$125. *Courtesy of Audrey and Joe Elsinger.*

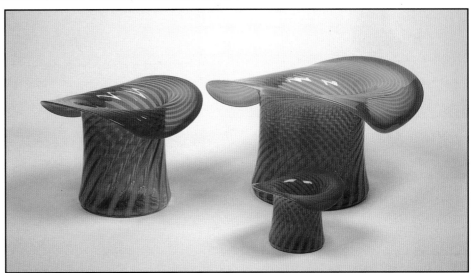

Opalescent - French Opalescent - Spiral Optic #1920 12" Top Hat, 1938. VALUE: $400-$500. *Courtesy of Emogene Snyder.*

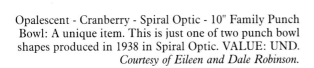

Opalescent - Cranberry - Spiral Optic - 10" Family Punch Bowl: A unique item. This is just one of two punch bowl shapes produced in 1938 in Spiral Optic. VALUE: UND. *Courtesy of Eileen and Dale Robinson.*

Opalescent - Cranberry - Spiral Optic - 8" Rose Bowl, circa 1938: A massive piece measuring 8" tall, shown next to the 5" tall Blue Ridge Squat Vase for comparison. VALUE: UND. *Courtesy of Linda and John Flippen.*

Opalescent - Green Opalescent - Spiral Optic - 8" Rose Bowl, circa 1938: Shown next to a 5" Rose Bowl for size comparison. VALUE: UND. *Courtesy of Jan Hollingsworth.*

Opalescent - Cranberry - Spiral Optic 12" Plate, circa 1938: Also known in this shape is a Blue Opalescent Plate. This plate was possibly used as an underliner for the Family Punch Bowl. VALUE: UND. *Author's Collection.*

Opalescent - Cranberry - Spiral Optic - Candy Dish/ Atomizer, circa 1938: The candy dish is a unique mould that has shown up only in Cranberry so far. The Atomizer was made for DeVilBiss and is also known in Blue Opalescent. VALUE: Candy: UND; Atomizer: $200-$250. *Courtesy of Linda and John Flippen.*

Opalescent - Cranberry - Spiral Optic - Candy Dish/Syrup, circa 1938: This Candy Dish is different from the one pictured previously, as it has the lid in the same pattern as the dish itself. Fenton commonly sold their candy dishes both ways, with a pattern lid and the #192 melon lid. They also used the #192 melon lid as a replacement lid, if someone would break a lid and order a new one. The glass part of the syrup was produced by Fenton, and then bought by another company and fitted with a plastic top. VALUE: UND. *Courtesy of Betty and Ike Hardman.*

Opalescent - Green Opalescent - Spiral Optic - Sugar Shaker/Syrup, 1940s: In all cases, previously, I have seen the Spiral Optic Syrups with the plastic lids, so I was mildly surprised when this one appear with a metal top. I was even more surprised to see its mate fitted with a metal shaker lid for a sugar shaker. VALUE: UND.

Opalescent - Green Opalescent - Spiral Optic - Syrup, circa 1938. VALUE: UND. *Courtesy of Alice and James Rose.*

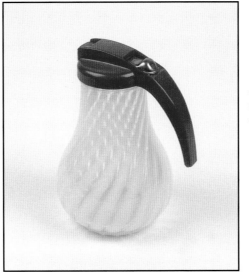

Opalescent - French Opalescent - Spiral Optic - Syrup, circa 1938. VALUE: UND. *Courtesy of Betty and Ike Hardman.*

Opalescent - Cranberry - Spiral Optic - Guest Set, 1938: In obtaining pictures for this book, besides the Hobnail pattern, it seems that I would run into more sample and Whimsey items in Spiral Optic. Of course, keep in mind that Spiral Optic was actually the first pattern for which Fenton produced anything in Opalescent, and remained so for a long while. So it is certain that they would sample many different moulds in, what at that time, was a new treatment. This is one that I'm sure many people wish that Fenton would have put into their regular line. This is now a very popular shape with collectors of early Fenton, and a very good seller when it's produced currently. VALUE: UND. *Courtesy of Emogene Snyder.*

Opalescent - Cranberry - #192 5.5" Jug: A very rare item in any color. It has been stated by some that this pattern in the #192 item was produced by Fenton for another company. VALUE: $100-$125. *Courtesy of Emogene Snyder.*

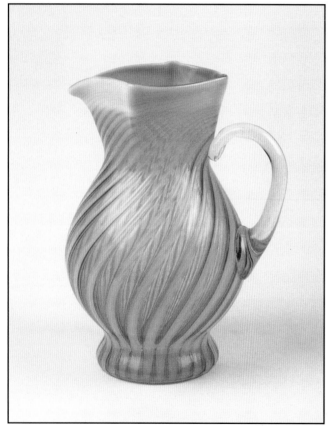

Opalescent - Cranberry Opalescent - Spiral Optic - #894 Jug, circa 1938. VALUE: UND. *Courtesy of Betty and Ike Hardman.*

Opalescent - Blu Opalescent - Spiral Optic - #183 Jug, circa 1938: Unique item, where the #183 10" Vase was adapted int a jug. VALUE: UND.

Opalescent - Blue Ridge - #187 Water Set, 1939: Needless to say, this jug is rare in any color! But to find it in Blue Ridge, and then also with the matching tumblers, is almost too much to imagine! VALUE: UND. *Courtesy of Charles Grigg.*

Opalescent - Green Opalescent - Spiral Optic – Lamp, 1938: It was unusual enough to find a lamp fashioned out of the Spiral Optic Rose Bowl; but, to also find one using the #170 Hurricane shape is almost unbelievable! VALUE: UND.

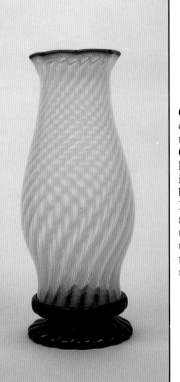

Opalescent - Blue Ridge - Spiral Optic - #170 Hurricane Lamp; 1938: It was in 1938, that Fenton started to go full force in the marketing and production of Opalescent Glass. Before this time, it had been in their line periodically. The two new colors made in the 1938 issue of Spiral Optic that had not been in Fenton's line before were Cranberry and Blue Ridge (which is French Opalescent with a Cobalt Rim). Cranberry has remained a mainstay color to this day. It is unfortunate that Blue Ridge has only had the 1938 issue and then the 1985 80th Anniversary issue. Not only was it one of the first Opalescent colors, it was also the first issue of the Crest line. VALUE: $300-$350.

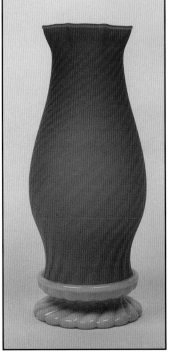

Opalescent - Cranberry Satin - Spiral Optic - #170 Hurricane Lamp, 1938: The collector needs to remember that it was only in 1953, and then only with the Fern, Diamond Optic, Rib Optic, and Swirled Feather, that Satinized Cranberry Opalescent was called Rose Satin. In all other cases, it should be referred to as Cranberry Satin. This lamp, along with other items satinized from the 1940s and 1950s, usually had a slight flaw and was satinized to cover it up. Keep in mind, this was many years before Fenton had their Gift Shop and outlet stores to dispose of the seconds. It is almost ironic that these items, in this treatment, many times command much higher prices than the glossy first quality items of the same time! VALUE: $250-$300.

Opalescent - Topa▊
Opalescent - Spira▊
Optic - 16" Lamp:
This is yet anothe▊
case where the lar▊
parts were made b▊
Fenton and offere▊
in their lamp
catalogs during th▊
1950s and 1960s,
then purchased ar▊
adapted into a lan▊
that was sold by
another individua▊
or company. Keep▊
mind, it wasn't un▊
the mid-1960s (wi▊
the Vasa Murrhin▊
Swag Lamp and
Mariner's Lamp
made from the sar▊
shape) that Fento▊
started to sell lam▊
themselves!
VALUE: $350+.

Opalescent - Cranberry Opalescent - Spiral Optic - 5" #183 Vase/#187 8" Vase/4" Special Rose Bowl: Three uncommon items. The #187 Vase was made off of one of the Barcelona moulds that Fenton bought from Diamond Glass Co. in the late 1930s. The #183 Vase is unusual as it was usually produced with a much longer neck, normally measuring 8" or 10". VALUE: #183 5" Vase: $150-$200; #187 Vase: $200-$250; Special Rose Bowl: $100-$150. *Courtesy of Linda and John Flippen.*

Opalescent - Cranberry - Spiral Optic - #893 Temple Jar Vase: Made off the Temple Jar mould. It's uncertain if this was a Whimsey item. VALUE: UND.

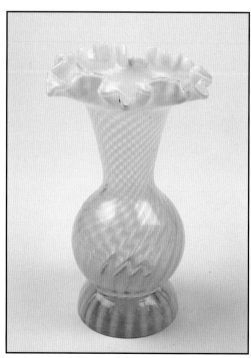

Opalescent - Green Opalescent - Spiral Optic - #184 11" Vase, 1938. VALUE: $200-$250.

Opalescent - French Opalescent - Spiral Optic - Weil Vase: This shape was produced in both Rose and Blue Overla▊ in the 1940s for Weil Ceramics. It's uncertain whether this shape was also made in French Opalescent in Spiral Optic for Weil or for Fenton. VALUE: UND. *Courtesy of Judy and Ckriss Cord.*

Opalescent - Blue - Spiral Optic - #187 9" Vase, 1938: Made off a Barcelona mould from the Diamond Glass Company after Fenton bought those moulds in the 1930s. VALUE: $225-$275. *Courtesy of Williamstown Antique Mall.*

Opalescent - Cranberry - Spiral Optic - #193 Hand Vase: This is a piece that is sure to make even the most jaded Cranberry collector sit up and take notice! VALUE: UND. *Courtesy of Alice and James Rose.*

Opalescent - French Opalescent - Spiral Optic - #3264 12" Vase: Made in the 1950s, at the same time this shape was produced in Cranberry. This color was definitely a sample item. VALUE: UND. *Author's Collection.*

Opalescent - Cranberry - Spiral Optic - #183 10" Vases: Both are very scarce items, but the vase with the boxed crimp is even more so. VALUE: Boxed Crimp: $250-$300; Tri Crimp: $150-$175. *Courtesy of Emogene Snyder.*

Opalescent - Cranberry - Rib Optic #1923 7" Basket: It's not sure when Fenton produced the Rib Optic Pattern, due to incomplete information and catalogs at the factory. It's fairly safe to say that it was in the late 1930s, at approximately the same time that Spiral Optic was made. All pieces in this pattern, in any color, are considered rare. VALUE: $200-$300. *Courtesy of Linda and John Flippen.*

Opalescent - French Opalescent - Rib Optic - #1924 Creamer: Like the Cranberry Spiral Optic Creamer pictured earlier, most serious collectors of Fenton still do not have this piece in their collections. VALUE: UND. *Courtesy of Betty and Ike Hardman.*

Opalescent - Cranberry - Rib Optic - #1522 12" Bowl. VALUE: $200-$250. *Courtesy of Linda and John Flippen.*

Opalescent - French Opalescent/ Cranberry - Rib Optic - #1924/ #1923/#1922/#1921 Top Hats: Seldom do you see a collection Top Hats in this pattern grouped together. This also verifies the assumption that, if an item made in either Cranberry Opalescent Rib Optic or French Opalescent Rib Optic appears, there is a good chance that it is out there in the other color. VALUE: #1924 4": $100-$125; #1923 7": $200-$225; #1922 9": UND; #1921 11": UND. *Courtesy of Linda and John Flippen.*

Opalescent - Cranberry - Rib Optic - 16" Lamp, circa late 1950s - early 1950s: Made from parts produced by Fenton and sold in their lamp catalog. VALUE: $400+. *Courtesy of Linda and John Flippen.*

Opalescent - Topaz Opalescent - Rib Optic -24" Lamp, circa late 1950s-early 1960s: This one puts the researcher in a twist! The fount and shade are definitely Fenton's, made at the same time as the previous two lamps. The Milk Glass foot is from L. G. Wright. This could be the result of one of two scenarios. A company could of purchased the glass pieces from both companies and assembled the lamp, or L. G. Wright could have purchased the Fenton glass pieces and used their own foot (which in this case was possibly manufactured by Fenton) and assembled the lamp. VALUE: $550+.

Opalescent - Topaz Opalescent - Rib Optic - 16" Lamp, circa late 1950s - early 1960s: Made from parts produced by Fenton and sold in their lamp catalog. VALUE: $400+. *Courtesy of Eileen and Dale Robinson.*

Opalescent - Cranberry - Rib Optic - #3001 8" Vase. VALUE: UND. *Courtesy of Lori and Michael Palmer.*

Opalescent - Blue Opalescent - Rib Optic - #201 5" Vase: Always keep in mind that any item in any color in Rib Optic is especially rare due to the very short period of production. It's not sure when this pattern was made by Fenton, or for how long, due to incomplete records and data at the factory. Many people believe, due to the colors and shapes that appear in it, that Rib Optic was produced in the late 1930s and early 1940s. VALUE: $80-$100. *Author's Collection.*

Opalescent - Cranberry - Rib Optic - 8" Vase, circa late 1950s-early 1960s: Bought at an estate auction of a former Fenton factory worker. Notice that this piece is the same shape as the #1766 Pitcher made in Diamond Optic in the Colonial colors during the 1960s. VALUE: UND.

Opalescent - Topaz Opalescent - Rib Optic - 1925 6" Vase: It's unclear when Fenton started to produce Topaz Opalescent. If you go by the introduction of that color in Hobnail, it will tell you that it was in July of 1940; but, with the appearance of it in Rib Optic and, going by all facts that Rib Optic was produced in 1938 when Spiral Optic was in production, it appears that Topaz Opalescent was in production by Fenton several years before. Whichever the case, it is rare in any pattern prior to its introduction in the Hobnail line in 1940. VALUE: $150-$200. *Courtesy of Alice and James Rose.*

Opalescent - Cranberry - Rib Optic 1950s - 7" Pinch Vase/4" Vase: Actually, the term for the color of the 7" Pinch Vase should be Glossy Rose, as this shape was originally produced in Rose Satin (Cranberry Satin) in the 1950s and was never marketed in the regular Cranberry Opalescent. As previously stated, in most cases, when an item was made regularly as a Satin Color, and appears in the Glossy color instead, it is referred to as "Glossy." The 4" Vase is a mystery as to when it was produced, although it is off the same mould used for the Creamer that was made in the Colonial colors in Diamond Optic in the mid-1960s. VALUE: UND. *Courtesy of Linda and John Flippen.*

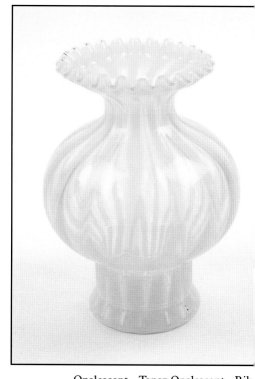

Opalescent - Topaz Opalescent - Rib Optic - Lamp Shade Vase: This vase is called a Lamp Shade Vase since, most of the time, the bottom was cut out of it to create a lamp shade. VALUE: UND. *Courtesy of Eileen and Dale Robinson.*

Opalescent - Cranberry Opaline - Rib Optic 1950s - #815 Cruet: Cranberry Opaline was a sample treatment which added more Opal in the formula to give the glass a cloudy effect. VALUE: UND. *Courtesy of Janice and Gordy Bowerman.*

Opalescent - Cranberry - Rib Optic - Handled Vase: Made from the same mould as the Handled Vase in Burmese Satin from the early 1970s. It's safe to assume that this piece was produced at that time, or shortly before, as it carries no logo. VALUE: UND. *Courtesy of Eileen and Dale Robinson.*

Opalescent - Glossy Lime Opaque - Rib Optic 1950s - #1720 7" Pinch Vase: I was completely bowled over when I found this piece, as nothing made in the 1950s in the Satin colors has ever appeared in Lime Satin, let alone in Lime Opaline, except for the Swirled Feather pattern. Since I'm such a Green lover, I had to take this one home! VALUE: UND. *Author's Collection.*

Opalescent - French Opalescent - Wide Rib Optic 1930s - Footed Ivy Ball: Made off the same moulds as the Ruby Overlay Dot Optic, Emerald Green Dot Optic, and Cranberry Opalescent Polka Dot Ivy Ball, this is the only one thus far to have a surface in Rib Optic. VALUE: UND. *Courtesy of Betty and Ike Hardman.*

Opalescent - Cranberry - Ring Optic- Cruet: During the late 1930s, when Spiral Optic was in production, Fenton produced a grouping of items called an "Unusual Opalescent Assortment." The Ring Pattern appeared in that grouping in several items. Listed only in French Opalescent, many of these items have since appeared in Cranberry, including this cruet. VALUE: UND. *Courtesy of Eileen and Dale Robinson.*

Opalescent - French Opalescent - Wide Rib Optic - #893 Ginger Jar, 1938: In 1938, at the onset of Fenton's main production of Opalescent glass, they introduced what they referred to in their catalogs as an "Unusual Opalescent Assortment." A wide variety of items appeared in this assortment, including several in Wide Rib Optic. As several of these shapes have surfaced in Cranberry since, it would pay the collector to keep an eye out for this shape in Cranberry. VALUE: $300-$400.

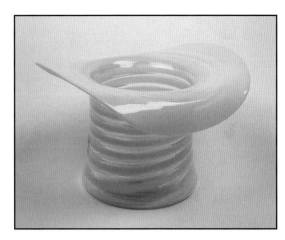

Opalescent - French Opalescent - Ring Optic - #1921 11" Top Hat. VALUE: $400+. *Courtesy of Linda and John Flippen.*

Opalescent - Rose Satin - Diamond Optic - #63 Large Covered Canister, 1952: This can be considered the mother of all Fenton rarities! Two have only been accounted for: the one large one pictured here and the small one that is currently in the Fenton Museum. Although pictured in a Fenton catalog and Made at the same time as the Diamond, Rib, Fern, and Swirled Feather Cruets, this canister did not survive in their line for very long. Most advance collectors of Fenton and Cranberry just wistfully dream of owning this piece. VALUE: UND. *Courtesy of Emogene Snyder.*

Opalescent - Lime Opalescent - Diamond Optic - #183 10" Vase, circa 1953. VALUE: $250-$300. *Courtesy of Williamstown Antique Mall.*

Opalescent - Cranberry - Ring Optic - Cruet/#510 8" Vase/#3005 11" Vase: Three very unusual items in a very scarce pattern. The cruet is the only one that might have been produced at the onset of Opalescent production in 1938. The others are moulds that became popular in the early 1940s and were sampled in this pattern. VALUE: UND.

Opalescent - Cranberry - Diamond Optic -11" Vase/#1925 6"
Vase: The Diamond Optic pattern is another that Fenton
produced (along with Rib Optic, Fern, and Feather Swirl) in
the Opalescent Satin colors in the 1950s. The 6" Vase is
another product that escaped the Satinizing process, and by
all technical terms would be called Glossy Rose. It's unknown when the 11" Vase was produced, but some of these
have been found with the indent in the bottom so a hole
could be drilled and are suspected that they were originally
Lamp Parts sold to other companies and fitted out to be
Lamps. VALUE: 11" Vase: $200-$250; 6" Vase: $150-$200.
Courtesy of Audrey and Joe Elsinger.

Opalescent - Cranberry - Diamond Optic/Daisy Optic - 7"
Lamp Fount Vases, circa 1960s: In most cases these pieces
were used for Lamp founts, but many were not drilled for
the electric cords and found their way into the Gift Shop to
be sold as Vases. VALUE: UND.

Opalescent - Cranberry -
Snowflake - 16" Lamp,
circa late 1950s. VALUE:
UND. *Courtesy of Audrey
and Joe Elsinger.*

Opalescent - Cranberry - Daisy Optic - Lamp Shade Vase: A very
unusual pattern produced by Fenton. It may have been made in the
1950s, as this shape for lamp shades was in use at that time.
However, the pattern itself was not made by Fenton and used in
their regular line until the 1990s, and was not in L. G. Wright's
line until the 1980s. VALUE: UND. *Courtesy of Betty and Ike
Hardman.*

Opalescent - Cranberry - Wedding Ring Optic - 16" Lamp, circa late 1950s. VALUE: UND. *Courtesy of Linda and John Flippen.*

Opalescent - Blue Opalescent/Topaz Opalescent - Drapery Opti #184 11" Vas circa 1938. VALUE: UN

Opalescent - French Opalescent - Priscilla - Water Goblet, early 1950s: This line was made by Fenton for such a short time that no sample colors or shapes have ever appeared before. VALUE: UND. *Courtesy of Millie Coty.*

Opalescent - Cranberry Opaline - Seaweed Optic - #510 8" Vase/#1720 7" Vase, circa 1953: This pattern was made as a sample, at the same time of the Satin Opalescent items, in Fern, Diamond Optic, and Rib Optic. Cranberry Opaline (and also Lime Opaline) was a sample treatment that added more Opal in the formula to give the glass a cloudy effect. VALUE: UND.

Opalescent - Lime Opaline - Seaweed Optic/Fern Optic - #1720 7" Vases, circa 1953: With the appearance of these vases in this treatment, and the knowledge of the presence of the Rib Optic and Fern Cruet, in Cranberry Opaline, it can only be hoped that these Cruets also might exist in Lime Opaline, and in the Seaweed Pattern in any color. VALUE: UND.

Opalescent - Cranberry Opaline - Fern Optic - #815 Cruet: 1953. VALUE: $300-$400+ *Author's Collection.*

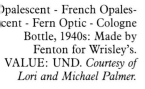

Opalescent - French Opalescent - Fern Optic - Cologne Bottle, 1940s: Made by Fenton for Wrisley's. VALUE: UND. *Courtesy of Lori and Michael Palmer.*

Opalescent - Cranberry - Speckled - #1924 Creamer: It's unsure what this treatment was actually called by Fenton; however, it was produced in various colors during the late part of the nineteenth century and the early part of the twentieth by Northwood and several other companies. Obviously, Fenton attempted to copy it and, either due to production difficulties or public reaction, abandoned it. VALUE: UND. *Courtesy of Alice and James Rose.*

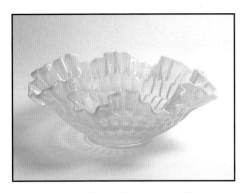

Opalescent - Topaz Opalescent - Thumbprint - 12" Bowl: Produced by Fenton in the early 1960s and sold through their Old Virginia Glass line. Any items in this color of Thumbprint are exceptionally rare. VALUE: UND. *Courtesy of Kill Creek Antiques.*

Opalescent - Topaz Opalescent - Thumbprint - 7" Basket/Comport/9" Basket/8" Vase/Bud Vase. VALUE: UND. *Courtesy of Kill Creek Antiques.*

Opalescent - Topaz Opalescent - Thumbprint - 6" Bonbon/7" Basket. VALUE: UND.

Opalescent - Topaz Opalescent - Thumbprint - Cake Plate. VALUE: UND. *Courtesy of Kill Creek Antiques.*

Opalescent - Topaz Opalescent - Thumbprint - Chip 'n' Dip.
VALUE: UND. *Courtesy of Kill Creek Antiques.*

Opalescent - Rib Optic – Ashtray, 1940s: Unique item with "Marietta Ohio Radio" advertising etched in the center. VALUE: $70-$80. *Courtesy of Lori and Michael Palmer.*

Opalescent - Rib Optic – Ashtray, 1940s: Close-up view of the etch.

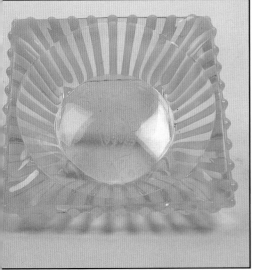

Opalescent - Cranberry - Thumbprint - 8" Vase: While Topaz Opalescent in Thumbprint was known to have been produced in the Old Virginia Glass line, there is no record of Cranberry being produced in Thumbprint. This piece might of been sampled at the same time that Thumbprint was in production in Topaz. VALUE: UND. *Courtesy of Linda and John Flippen.*

Opalescent - Blue Opalescent - 11" Swan Handled Bowl, 1938: Fenton made a variety of these Swan bowls in the late 1930s in Crystal, Crystal Satin, and Milk Glass. This bowl is possibly a sample made at a time that this mould was in production, at the onset of Opalescent production by Fenton. VALUE: UND.

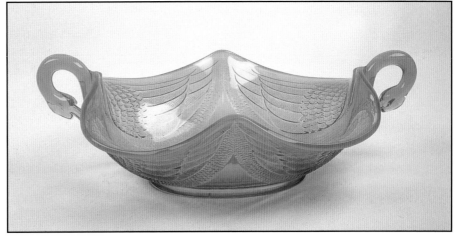

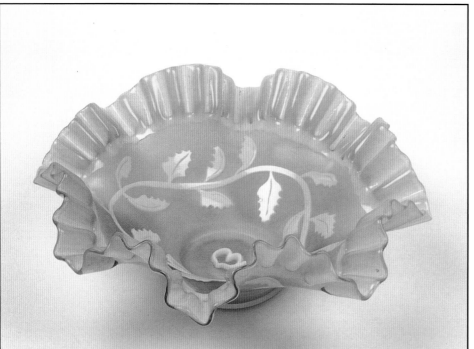

Overlay - Rose Overlay - #1522 10" Sand-blasted Design Bowl, circa 1940s: While some sandblasting/carving has been done by Fenton in the past twenty years, none has ever surfaced before that, until this time. This bowl is unique and resembles Cameo Glass, which, in effect—since this is Overlay glass—it is! VALUE: UND. *Courtesy of Andrea Calhoun.*

Overlay - Rose Overlay - 10" Sandblasted Design Bowl.

Overlay - Blue Overlay - #7269 Cruet: This shape has not appeared in any other Fenton treatment, except for Silver, Emerald, and Aqua Crest. It dates from the early 1950s. VALUE: UND. *Courtesy of Betty and Ike Hardman.*

Overlay - Blue Overlay - Cruet: This cruet dates several years before the previously pictured Cruet, possibly back to the early to mid-1940s. VALUE: UND. *Courtesy of Betty and Ike Hardman.*

Overlay - Blue Overlay with Gold Crest - #192 Melon Cruet, circa 1943: As I have stated many times before, as you go out each day, you will never know what will come across your path! I found this piece at the Flea Market in Williamstown Park during the 2001 Fenton Convention. VALUE: UND. *Author's Collection.*

Overlay - Blue/Rose Overlay - #192 Melon Cruets: Although not in the regular Fenton line, this shape cruet surfaces periodically. Maybe made for another individual, such as Weil, this shape also exists in Peach Crest, Ruby Overlay, and Mulberry, which would date all of them back to 1942. VALUE: $125-$150 each. *Author's Collection.*

Overlay - Blue Overlay #1923 7" Creamer/Milk Pitcher: ictured next to the regular 4" #1924 Creamer for size comparison, this Milk Pitcher is much larger. Probably made in the 940s as a sample item. VALUE: UND. *Courtesy of Betty and Ike Hardman.*

Overlay - Rose Overlay - #203 Squat Creamer: Made in the 1940s, possibly for another company such as Weil Ceramics. VALUE: UND. *Author's Collection.*

Overlay - Blue Overlay - Beaded Melon 6" Plate: This should send the Beaded Melon collectors into a tail spin! It is not know whether this was an underliner to a mayonnaise set or was just produced as a simple plate. VALUE: UND. *Courtesy of Caryl Graham.*

Overlay - Rose Overlay - #192 Whimsey Creamer: Made from the #192 5.5" Jug mould, with the neck cut down and flared more than the regular 5.5" Jug. VALUE: UND. *Courtesy of Betty and Ike Hardman.*

Overlay - Rose Overlay - Weil 9" Jug: Made for Weil Ceramics, also made in Blue Overlay. This piece is also know in a vase form. VALUE: $100-$125. *Author's Collection.*

Overlay - Blue Overlay - #192 8" Melon Bank: This has to be a worker's pet, and as Frank Fenton puts it, "Walked out in a lunch box." I have only seen one other Fenton item made into a bank over the years of my collecting. VALUE: UND. *Author's Collection.*

Overlay - Rose Overlay - #192 Ring Tree?: Obviously a Whimsey item made in the early 1940s during the production of Rose Overlay. VALUE: UND. *Courtesy of Thomas K. Smith.*

Overlay - Blue Overlay - DeVilBiss Atomizer/ Atomizer Vase, 1940s: Fenton produced a large number of items for DeVilBiss to adapt into Atomizers and Perfumes in the 1940s, including this shape, in Blue Overlay, Peach Crest, and Rose Overlay. During the same period, this shape was also sold as a vase, either by DeVilBiss or another company that Fenton produced glass for. VALUE: Atomizer: $125-$150; Vase: $80-$100. *Author's Collection.*

Overlay - Rose Overlay - #711 Beaded Melon 8" Lamp/#1721 8" Pinch Vase: This is a case where you never, ever say never. It's been stated many times that Beaded Melon can not exist in Rose Overlay, as Rose Overlay had been discontinued for several years prior to the introduction of the Beaded Melon pattern. This is a good case where a soon to be discontinued color/treatment was used to sample a soon to be released pattern/mould. The 8" Pinch Vase was first thought to have been adapted from a vase that Frank Fenton bought at an Antique show in the very early 1950s. Either this example in Rose Overlay was made much later, in an attempt to bring back the color, or the mould was made much earlier than originally thought. VALUE: UND. *Author's Collection.*

Overlay - Blue Overlay - #194 13" Vase. VALUE:
UND. *Courtesy of Laurie and Richard Karman.*

Overlay - Rose
Rose/Rose Satin
Overlay - #193 11"
Hand Vases: These
Hand Vases has
popped up in more
different Fenton
colors and treat-
ments over the past
few years than first
was thought
possible. Most seem
to date from around
1942-43. VALUE:
$250-$300 each.
*Courtesy of Eileen
and Dale Robinson.*

Overlay - Goldenrod - 10" Bowl: Now, to confuse the collector even more
when distinguishing Goldenrod from Yellow and Amber Overlay! Goldenrod
was listed in Fenton catalogs in only seven items in 1956. For years, no other
items, samples, or whimseys have appeared in that color. (Keep in mind that
it was only made for six months!) A 6" Hobnail Vase is pictured in my book,
Fenton Glass Compendium 1940-70, that, due to the deeper color, was determined to have been a sample item. Since that book came out, this 10" Bowl
has surfaced. VALUE: UND. *Courtesy of Eileen and Dale Robinson.*

Overlay - Green/Amber Overlay - #815 Cruets: When you go
to do a project such as this, and have the opportunity to see
some of the larger collections of Fenton, it sometimes is
surprising to see what comes out of these collections. Such is
the case here. This shape was very much in the Fenton line at
the same time as these two colors; but, until now it was never
know that this color and shape were put together. The #815
Cruet in Ivy Overlay has been documented as being produced
for Abels Wasserberg for use with their Charleton decoration.
VALUE: UND. *Courtesy of Alice and James Rose.*

Overlay - Green Overlay - #1921 Top Hat: Made in the late 1930s with a matching glass cane. Very Rare. VALUE: UND. *Courtesy of Betty and Ike Hardman.*

Overlay - Ivy - #93 Candy Dish: I think, out of all the pieces I own, that this has to be one of my favorites, as it isn't only in one of my favorite colors, but also one of my favorite shapes. Made as a sample item in the early 1950s. VALUE: UND. *Author's Collection.*

Overlay - Ivy - #93 Candy Dish: Notice, in this picture, how the inner layer of Milk Glass did not cover the outer layer of Green.

Overlay - Jamestown Transparent - Flat Ivy Ball, circa late 1950s. VALUE: UND. *Author's Collection.*

Overlay - Blown Out Peach Blow - #1522 10" Bowl, circa early 1940s: Many advanced and serious Fenton collectors, when they looked at this piece, did not think it was Fenton and could not comprehend how it was made. I was not sure myself until Frank Fenton explained to me how it was created. In layman's terms, a ball of crystal is gathered over Ruby and then gathered over Opal (Milk Glass), in the same way that Peach Blow/Peach Crest is formed. Then, instead of blowing it on through to create Peach Blow, the bubble of Ruby Glass was popped, which made the ring of Pink glass in the bowl. This treatment, according to Frank Fenton, was sampled at the same time that Peach Crest was being sampled, and proved too time consuming to make. VALUE: UND. *Author's Collection.*

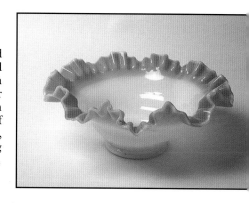

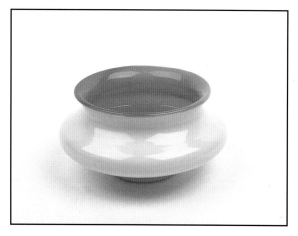

Overlay - Peach Blow - 4" Special Rose Bowl: A very unusual lip, with an extra wide opening, for this little Rose Bowl. VALUE: $75-$100. *Author's Collection.*

Overlay - Peach Blow - #711 Beaded Melon Creamer: I have yet to figure out whether this was actually made as Peach Blow, or was intended as Peach Crest and the crest was left off. According to Frank Fenton, in some cases, with some moulds, it was impossible to apply the crests, as they would pop off as soon as they were applied. This might be the case here, as I have never seen this piece in actual Peach Crest, although it is on the price lists. Also, this shape has never appeared in other crested Beaded Melon colors! Several others like this one has surfaced since it was pictured in the *Big Book of Fenton 1940-70.* VALUE: UND. *Author's Collection.*

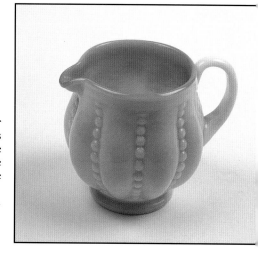

Overlay - Peach Blow - 10" Vase: An unusual item, as this was later known as an L. G. Wright shape used in many of their Opalescent patterns as a pitcher. See, in the following picture, the 1930s era Fenton Sample Sticker. VALUE: UND.

Overlay - Peach Blow - 10" Vase Sticker.

Overlay - Peach Blow - #1924 Tall Vase: At first I thought it possible that this might be a sugar, as it is the exact same size and height as the Peach Crest and Overlays #1924 Creamer. However, a Peach Blow Creamer has never surfaced. VALUE: UND.

Overlay - Peach Blow - Jacqueline - #9152 7" Vase, circa early 1960s: Actually referred to as Milk Glass with a Wild Rose interior. When you see a piece of this beside Peach Crest, you will know the difference!! This is the exact reverse of the Wild Rose Overlay, which was made in the early 1960s. VALUE: UND. *Author's Collection.*

Overlay - Peach Blow - Spanish Lace - #3551 7" Vase, circa early 1960s: Made on the same formula as the above Jacqueline Vase, it looks very much like the Peach Crest Spanish Vase pictured earlier. VALUE: UND. *Courtesy of Williamstown Antique Mall.*

Overlay - Peach Blow on Ivory - #204 5" Vase: Originally from the Rosenthal Collection, and sold at a FAGCA Auction several years ago. This interesting piece is Peach Blow, but not on regular Milk Glass. It is on Custard, using the same base as Ivory Crest was made on. VALUE: UND. *Courtesy of Cindy and Rick Blais.*

Overlay - Plated Amberina - 8" Basket: It's surprising to me that a color that was so briefly in the Fenton line could have so many Whimsey and sample items surface in it. Either the workers at the factory must have loved this color, while making it, or had a hard time getting it to come out the way they wanted it! Enjoy the next few pictures, as I have never seen any of these items anywhere else in this color! VALUE: UND.
Courtesy of Eileen and Dale Robinson.

Overlay - Plated Amberina - Basket/6" Vase: Possible sample items, notice the different type of crimp on the basket. The vase could have been produced for a lamp part. VALUE: UND. *Courtesy of Chuck Bingham.*

Overlay - Plated Amberina - #1761 32 oz. Jug. VALUE: UND. *Courtesy of Eileen and Dale Robinson.*

Overlay - Plated Amberina - 10" Bowl. VALUE: UND. *Courtesy of Eileen and Dale Robinson.*

Overlay - Plated Amberina - #1921 Top Hat. VALUE: UND. *Courtesy of Linda and John Flippen.*

Overlay - Plated Amberina - #1780 Candy Box. VALUE: 200-$250. *Courtesy of Eileen and Dale Robinson.*

Overlay - Plated Amberina - #193 Hand Vase: Earlier I stated that most of these Hand Vases were produced in the 1942 period. As I have stated many times, never say never. A few popped up in treatments made much later on, such as this one from 1963. VALUE: UND. *Courtesy of Eileen and Dale Robinson.*

Overlay - Plated Amberina - #711 6" Jug with Crest/#6457 7" Fan Vase/#3752 11" Hobnail Vase. VALUE: UND. *Courtesy of Eileen and Dale Robinson.*

Overlay - Mulberry - #192 Oil Lamp: Close-up of Lamp without burner.

Overlay - Mulberry - #37 Mini Vase/Creamer: This is sure to send the serious Mini Vase and Creamer collector out in hot pursuit! VALUE: UND. *Courtesy of Eileen and Dale Robinson.*

Overlay - Mulberry - #192 Oil Lamp: Made off the same mould as the previously pictured Blue Overlay and Rose Overlay Cruets, this item was sold to another company and was fitted with a burner. VALUE: UND. *Courtesy of Eileen and Dale Robinson.*

Overlay - Mulberry - #192 8" Vase: Notice the unique straight edge crimp. Few examples are know to exist with this crimp. VALUE: UND. *Courtesy of Betty and* Hardman.

Overlay - Mulberry - Long Neck Cruet/Decanter: The cruet is obviously a Whimsey, made from the #192 5.5" cologne. The decanter was reported to have been made for another individual out of New York who, after one turn of the bottle was made, decided not to buy it. No others were made. It is reported that approximately 25 of these are known to exist! VALUE: UND. *Courtesy of Eileen and Dale Robinson.*

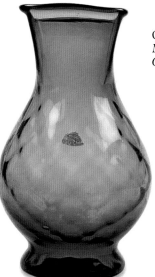

Overlay - Mulberry - #895 10" Vase: Unlisted shape in the Mulberry color. Possibly a sample item. VALUE: UND. *Courtesy of Ike and Betty Hardman.*

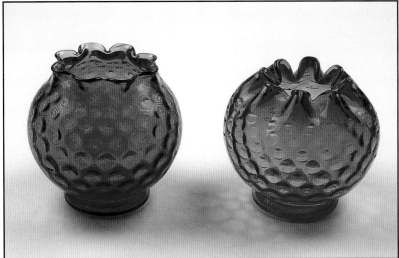

Overlay - Ruby Overlay/Blue - Decanter/Decanter: This cologne somehow missed out on the overlay process, never receiving a Milk Glass core (used to make Blue Overlay), and ended up transparent Blue. (A Ruby Core was used to make Mulberry.) It is not known how the Ruby Overlay Decanter came into being, as there is no records of it being made in this color. Keep in mind that this piece is over 10" tall and approximately 5.5" diameter at the widest point. VALUE: UND. *Courtesy of Alex James; Decanter; Author's Collection.*

Overlay - Ruby Overlay – Cruet, 1940s. VALUE: $125-$150. *Courtesy of Lori and Michael Palmer.*

Overlay - Ruby Overlay - Thumbprint - Star Crimped Rose Bowl: Comparison with the regular production Rose Bowl.

Overlay - Ruby Overlay - Thumbprint - #2424 Star Crimped Rose Bowl. VALUE: UND. *Author's Collection.*

129

Overlay - Ruby Overlay - Thumbprint - #2467 Water Pitcher/ #2447 Tumbler: Made only in 1956 in the Ruby Overlay Thumbprint Pattern. This is the only time that this shape was used by Fenton. Also, this is the first time that they called an item a pitcher; before that, they were referred to as jugs. The tumbler is an example where an older mould is brought back and put into use. VALUE: Pitcher: $200-$250; Tumbler: $55-$65. *Author's Collection.*

Overlay - Powder Blue Overlay - Bubble Optic - Bowl/Vase: Many times this shape would be produced for use as a lamp shade by cutting out the bottom of the piece. Made for the B. & P. Lamp Company of Tennessee. VALUE: UND. *Courtesy of Eileen and Dale Robinson.*

Overlay - Ruby Overlay Satin - Thumbprint - #2456 6" Ring Neck Vase: During the 1940s to 1970s, Fenton would occasionally use the satinizing process on items that would have been deemed seconds, in the hopes that this process would hide whatever flaw was in the item. This item would then usually be sold at the Gift Shop. Also keep in mind that Fenton's Gift Shop did not come into being until the late 1950s. VALUE: $75-$85. *Courtesy of Linda and John Flippen*

Overlay - Wild R[...] - Bubble Optic - Bowl/Vase: Made [...] for the B. & P. Lamp Company [...] Tennessee. VALU[...] UND. *Courtesy of Noralee and Ralp[...] Rogers.*

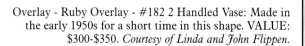

Overlay - Ruby Overlay - #182 2 Handled Vase: Made in the early 1950s for a short time in this shape. VALUE: $300-$350. *Courtesy of Linda and John Flippen.*

Overlay - Honey Amber - Bubble Optic - #1353 70 oz. Jug: Made for the B. & P. Lamp Company in the early 1960s. VALUE: $150-$200. *Courtesy of Eileen and Dale Robinson.*

Overlay - Honey Amber - 11" Vase, circa mid-1960s: A very unusual item which has never popped up before in #7251 Bubble Optic in this shape, either in this or any other color. VALUE: UND. *Courtesy of Douglas Smith.*

Overlay - Honey Amber - Jacqueline- #9153 5" Vase, circa 1960: When the Opaline colors in Jacqueline were discontinued, so were the two shapes that were produced in the Opaline colors, including this 5" size. The following year, when Jacqueline was made in Overlay colors, it was produced in completely new shapes. It's very unusual for this size of Jacqueline vase to appear in any of the Overlay colors. VALUE: $65-$75.

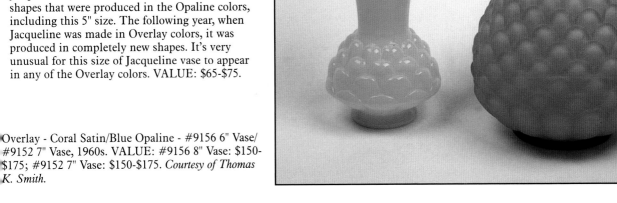

Overlay - Coral Satin/Blue Opaline - #9156 6" Vase/ #9152 7" Vase, 1960s. VALUE: #9156 8" Vase: $150-$175; #9152 7" Vase: $150-$175. *Courtesy of Thomas K. Smith.*

Overlay - Honey Amber - Wild Rose & Bowknot - Squat Jug: While this item was listed in Milk Glass in the Fenton catalogs during the first part of the 1960s, no records indicate that it was ever made in any of the Overlay colors. VALUE: UND. *Courtesy of Williamstown Antique Mall.*

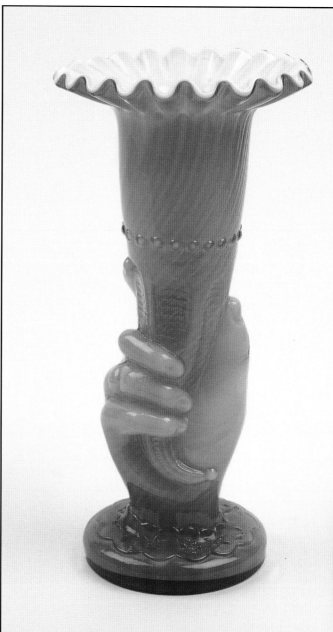

Overlay - Wild Rose - Candy Box: Oh, now to find the lid to this little jewel! Made as a sample item in the 1960s. VALUE: UND. *Courtesy of Eileen and Dale Robinson.*

Overlay - Wild Rose - #193 Hand Vase: Just when you think that you know of every color in this shape, another one pops up! Made as a sample item in the early 1960s. VALUE: UND. *Courtesy of Eileen and Dale Robinson.*

Overlay - Vasa Murrhina - #6435 7" Baskets/#6437 11" Baskets: Out of all the items that Fenton sampled in the 1940s-70s, I think that the workers had the most fun with the Vasa Murrhina treatment. More items, in various color combinations, have appeared in this treatment than in any of the other Fenton Sample items! Keep in mind that before Fenton recreated the formula/process to make Vasa Murrhina, it had been lost for over 100 years. I believe that the time it took to recreate this treatment, in part, explains why so many different color combinations and variations have appeared. Also, the success of this treatment paved the way for Fenton to recreate Burmese, Roselane, and Blue Burmese. Notice the one basket on the right in this picture, where even the handle was given the Vasa treatment. Most of the items in Vasa Murrhina, in the following pictures, come out of the same collection—probably one of the most comprehensive collections of Fenton ever assembled. VALUE: UND. *Courtesy of Betty and Ike Hardman.*

Overlay - Vasa Murrhina - Autumn - #1605 New World Shakers: Again, an item that never made it into regular production. It seemed that, due to the demand of earth tone colors in the mid-1960s, Fenton had more success with the Autumn Vasa Murrhina than any of the other colors. VALUE: UND. *Courtesy of Carolyn and Dick Grable.*

Overlay - Vasa Murrhina - Fairy Lights: The first fairy light that Fenton produced was in Hobnail in the late 1960s. Soon they were making them in every pattern that they produced. These two fairy lights show evidence that they sampled the shape in the mid-1960s when Vasa Murrhina was in the line. VALUE: UND. *Courtesy of Betty and Ike Hardman.*

Overlay - Vasa Murrhina - Bank, circa 1965: In all the years that I have dealt in Fenton, I have only seen two banks made from Fenton Vases. Fortunately, I am the proud owner of the Blue Overlay Bank, pictured earlier, and wish I had this one in my greedy little hand! This is a very unusual shape to begin with, and having the crimp folded over to make the slot for the bank makes it even more so. VALUE: UND. *Courtesy of Betty and Ike Hardman.*

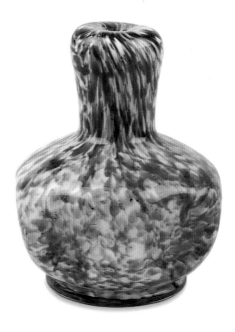

Overlay - Vasa Murrhina - Footed Rose Bowl. VALUE: UND. *Courtesy of Susie, Tiffany and Ron Ballard.*

Overlay - Vasa Murrhina #1923 7" Top Hat. VALUE: UND. *Courtesy of Betty and Ike Hardman.*

Overlay - Vasa Murrhina - Creamer/Tumbler/Flower Pot: This is *not* the bottom part of the handle on the creamer; it *is* another example of the workers getting funny after hours! The Tumbler is made from the Fan Vase, out of the Sear's/Vincent Price Series from 1967. The flower pot was derived from the 12" Vase. VALUES: UND. *Courtesy of Betty and Ike Hardman.*

Overlay - Vasa Murrhina - #6456 8" Vase: Very unusual color combination. VALUE: UND. *Courtesy of Eileen and Dale Robinson.*

Overlay - Vasa Murrhina - #6452 7" Fan Vase. VALUE: UND. *Courtesy of Betty and Ike Hardman.*

Overlay - Vasa Murrhina - #6452 7" Fan Vase. VALUE: UND. *Courtesy Betty and Ike Hardman.*

Overlay - Vasa Murrhina - #6464 4" Vases. VALUE: UND. *Courtesy of Betty and Ike Hardman.*

Overlay - Vasa Murrhina - 8" Vase. VALUE: UND. *Courtesy of Betty and Ike Hardman.*

overlay - Vasa Murrhina - 6" Vases/7" Vases/ " Creamer: A good example of some 1970s ra moulds that were being put to use some years earlier as sample items. VALUE: UND. *Courtesy of Betty and Ike Hardman.*

Overlay - Vasa Murrhina - 11" Vase: A unique color combination, Honey Amber with Green Flecks. VALUE: UND. *Courtesy of Carolyn and Dick Grable.*

Overlay - Kitchen Green Overlay - 9" Weil Jug: Very unusual Overlay color, possibly made along with Rose and Blue Overlay in the early 1940s for Weil Ceramics. VALUE: UND. *Author's Collection.*

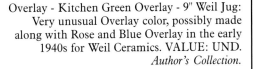

Overlay - Wild Rose Overlay (Early) - #203 4" Vase: Obviously Fenton experimented with the Wild Rose Overlay in the 1940s before they produced it in the early 1960s. Frank Fenton not only has several items in this Overlay in his private collection, but also one that was triple cased in blue, giving it a Mulberry cast. VALUE: UND. *Author's Collection.*

Overlay - Rubina Verde - #711 6" Beaded Melon Jug: This item looks like an early attempt at making Rubina Verde. Nearly fifty years later, it would finally be successfully produced by Fenton. VALUE: UND. *Courtesy of Betty and Ike Hardman.*

Overlay - Unknown Color Attempt - #37 Mini Basket: It is hard to judge by looking at this piece just what color this was suppose to have been. It honestly looks like an early attempt at making Cranberry in a pressed mould! VALUE: UND. *Courtesy of Eileen and Dale Robinson.*

Overlay - Unknown Color Attempt - Custard Slag with Pink Rim - Ring Neck Vase, circa 1950s?: In this sample, the workers at Fenton went all out to try something different. This piece was made in the same way as the Blown Out Peach Blow Bowl. This time Custard was cased with Ruby Glass, and the bubble of Ruby was popped to give it the ring around the edge of the vase. In doing this, it gave the rest of the vase a slag effect. It was then decorated on the neck with Gold paint. As has been stated before, the process to make Blown Out Peach Blow proved to be too time consuming and this treatment was quickly abandon. VALUE: UND. *Courtesy of Millie Coty.*

Overlay - Unknown Color Attempt - Milk Glass with Pink Slag - #192 Squat Jug, circa 1940s: This piece was actually found years ago at the Fenton Factory on the Slag Pile! Growing up down the street from the factory does have it advantages, doesn't it Millie? VALUE: UND. *Courtesy of Millie Coty.*

Overlay - Unknown Color Attempt - Milk Glass with Pink Slag - #192 Squat Jug, circa 1940s. UND.

Chapter Seven

Pastel Milk Glass/Milk Glass/Transparent Items

Transparent - Clear with Lime Crest /Clear Dot Optic: #711 6" Melon Vase: No records exist to indicate when these treatments were produced, or what they were to have been called. VALUE: UND. *Author's Collection.*

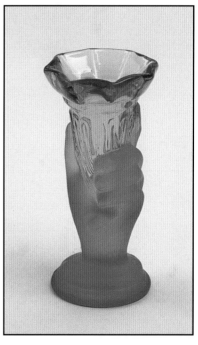

Transparent - No Opalescent Blue - Mini Hand Vase, 1942: I thought I had really found something "unique" with the No Opalescent Blue Mini Hand Vase pictured above, but this one tops it, as the hand part of the vase is satinized. This may have been an attempt to dress up this item, since it had to be produced without the bone ash necessary to make the Opalescent. VALUE: UND. *Courtesy of Lori and Michael Palmer.*

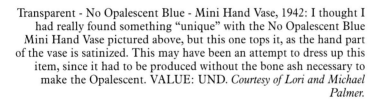

Transparent - #37 No Opalescent Blue - Mini Vases/Baskets: It was never thought possible that any of the mini items would have been produced in the No Opalescent Blue color. For those of you that have not read my previous book, *Fenton Glass Compendium 1940-70*, the No Opalescent Blue color came into being during WWII when bone ash could not be obtained to make Opalescent. When that happened, glass was produced without the bone ash in plain transparent colors. Hobnail is one pattern that appears frequently in the No Opalescent colors. This is the first indication that other items were produced without bone ash during this time period. VALUE: UND. *Courtesy of Mary Knight.*

Transparent - Green/Blue - Butterfly Net - Mini Vase/Mini Basket: In the early 1940s, Fenton produced a line of dinnerware for a short time for another company. This pattern, called the Butterfly Net, featured plates and cups & saucers. Each was decorated with an embossed Butterfly that looked to be hanging in an all-over net pattern. These two items were produced as accessory items to go along with this pattern. VALUE: UND. *Courtesy of Fenton Glass Museum.*

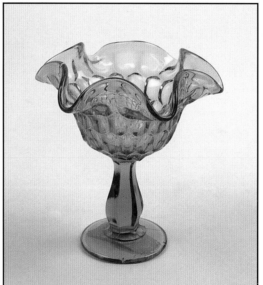

Transparent - Blue - Thumbprint - Comport, circa early 1960s: Possibly a sample item to have been introduced in the Old Virginia Glass Line. VALUE: $55-$65. *Author's Collection.*

Transparent - Blue - Thumbprint - Decanter; early 1960s: Possibly made to sell in the Old Virginia Glass line, this decanter pops up from time to time. VALUE: $300-$350. *Author's Collection.*

Transparent - Blue - Thumbprint - Decanter Jack in the Pulpit Vase, early 1960s: Possibly a sample item to have been introduced in the Old Virginia Glass Line. VALUE: UND. *Courtesy of Betty and Ike Hardman.*

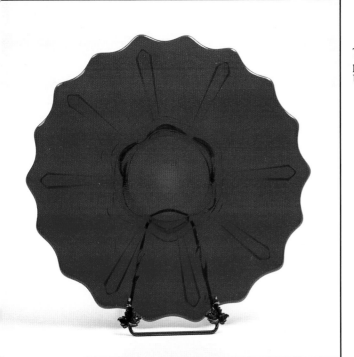

Transparent - Ruby - Cactus - #3411 Plate, circa 1960s: Made possibly as a sample item for Old Virginia Glass. VALUE: UND. *Courtesy of Trudy and Dick Green.*

Transparent - Amber - Daisy & Button - Top Hat Salt Shaker, circa late 1930s: Although this falls a little out of the time frame for this book, this piece was too good to past up. This item is seldom seen and few collectors realize that it was made by Fenton. VALUE: $50-$60 each. *Courtesy of Millie Coty.*

Milk Glass - Hobnail Decorated - Abel's Wasserberg Decorated - 5.5" Basket: Most of the Abel's Wasserberg items were produced on Crest. It's very unusual to have an item such as this surface in Hobnail. Also unusual is the fact that this delicate Violet pattern would later be the inspiration for the Fenton's Violets in the Snow decoration. VALUE: UND. *Author's Collection.*

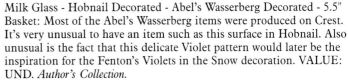

Milk Glass - Hobnail Decorated - Abel's Wasserberg Decorated - 5.5" Basket. VALUE: UND.

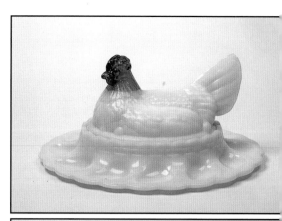

Milk Glass - Black - Cruet: Made in the 1950s, possibly as a sample item. VALUE: UND. *Courtesy of Eileen and Dale Robinson.*

Milk Glass - Black/White - White/Transparent Green - Ivy Balls: The Black & White Ivy Ball was possibly sampled, in anticipation of its sale when the Dawn treatment in the New World pattern was in production. The Green & White Ivy Ball has the unique Dot & Miter Pattern that both Fenton & L. G. Wright had trouble producing. VALUE: UND. *Courtesy of Betty and Ike Hardman.*

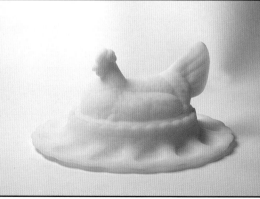

Milk Glass - Black/White - #5156 Fish Vases: Very rare! Although in production for almost a year in the 1950s, these two vases seldom come on the market! VALUE: $1,000+ each. *Courtesy of Gordy and Janice Bowerman.*

Opposite page:
Right top to bottom;
Milk Glass - White with Green Head - #5188 Hen Server. VALUE: $400+. *Courtesy of Carolyn and Dick Grable.*

Milk Glass - White with Black Head - #5188 Hen Server. VALUE: $400+. *Courtesy of LuAnn and Atlee Beene.*

Milk Glass - Amethyst/White Head - #5188 Hen Server. VALUE: $400+. *Courtesy of LuAnn and Atlee Beene.*

Milk Glass - White - #5188 Hen Server: Rare in the regular Green/White or Amethyst/White combination, this Chicken Server is extremely rare in White Satin. VALUE: $400+. *Courtesy of Twins Antiques.*

Milk Glass - Rose Pastel - Cologne Bottles: Made in the 1950s off the Swirled Feather cologne bottle mould. VALUE: UND. *Courtesy of Janice and Gordy Bowerman.*

Milk Glass - Kitchen Green - Vase: Produced for the E. T. Paul Company in the 1940s to be turned into a lamp. Also known in an Opaque Blue similar to the Glossy Blue Satin of the 1970s VALUE: $50-$65. *Author's Collection.*

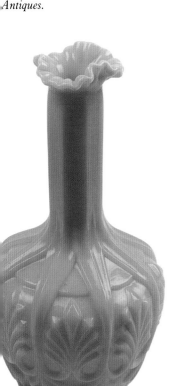

Milk Glass - Rose Pastel - 15.5" Plate. VALUE: UND. *Author's Collection.*

Milk Glass - Turquoise - #193 Hand Vase: Another exceptionally rare item, possibly a sample from the 1950s VALUE: UND. *Courtesy of Eileen and Dale Robinson.*

141

Chapter Eight

Items Made for Other Companies

DeVilBiss Atomizers 1940s-1950s

During the Second World War, when it became impossible for different companies and wholesalers to get glassware from overseas, Fenton and many other American companies filled the void. One of the major companies that bought glass from Fenton at this time was DeVilBiss of Toledo, Ohio. Formed in 1888, one of their workers created the atomizer and the company later patented the idea. At first they bought glassware from companies such as Hawkes, Heisey, Cambridge, and others; but, soon DeVilBiss found it more profitable to buy glass from overseas, import it, and fit it with their atomizers.

During the war, importation came to a stop and DeVilBiss turned to Fenton for their source of bottles for their atomizers. Fenton cooperated and first developed their Hobnail Mini Vase into a bottle. Later the Hobnail Mini Vase was followed by bottles in other patterns, such as Pine Cone, Plumes, Pearls, Petticoats, Ball shaped bottles in Dot Optic, a lovely tall bottle in Spiral Optic, and later still, the same shape in Coin Dot. The association with DeVilBiss continued for several years after the war; but, by the early 1950s they again had turned to the cheaper European imports.

DeVilBiss - Cranberry - Beads Atomizer: As the popularity of the Fenton produced DeVilBiss Atomizers rose, and supplies from glass companies overseas either were halted or dwindled due to the Second World War, Fenton started to produce special patterns for DeVilBiss. The Beads pattern, along with the Embossed Mini Flowers (called by some Cosmos) and Pinecone vase, was one of the new patterns that was developed exclusively for DeVilBiss. VALUE: $250-$300. *Courtesy of Linda and John Flippen.*

DeVilBiss - Topaz Opalescent - Petticoats Atomizer Bottle Adapted into an Oil Lamp: Many of the Atomizer bases that were made for DeVilBiss were adapted into Mini Oil Lamps. It's not known whether DeVilBiss did this or, when they had a surplus of these at Fenton, whether another company came in and bought them to make into Oil Lamps. VALUE: $200-$250.

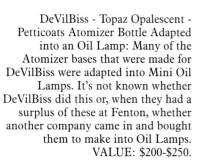

DeVilBiss - Blue Opalescent - Paneled Scroll Atomizer, circa 1940s. VALUE: $200-$250.

DeVilBiss - Green Opalescent - Pine Cone Atomizer Adapted Oil Lamp. VALUE: $200-$250. *Courtesy of Eileen and Dale Robinson.*

Overlay - Blue/Rose Overlay - DeVilBiss Atomizer Bottles, made in the late 1940s: Although this shape of Atomizer was on the market for several years, you seldom see one now. A very unusual trio. VALUE: UND. *Courtesy of Lori and Michael Palmer.*

DeVilBiss - Blue Opalescent - Mini Flowers (Cosmos) Atomizer Vase Whimsey: Made from an Atomizer base. VALUE: UND. *Courtesy of Betty and Ike Hardman.*

DeVilBiss - Topaz Opalescent - Mini Flowers (Cosmos) Atomizer Vase Whimsey: Made from an Atomizer base. VALUE: UND.

DeVilBiss - Blue Opalescent - Plumes Atomizer Vase Whimsey: Made from an Atomizer base. VALUE: UND. *Courtesy of Lori and Michael Palmer.*

L. G. Wright Glass Company 1930s-1990s

The L. G. Wright Glass Company, formed by Si Wright in 1937, had a close working relationship with the Fenton Art Glass Company for over sixty years. Si Wright had originally worked as salesperson with the New Martinsville Glass Company before branching out on his own in 1937. Shortly before his departure from New Martinsville, he had several opportunities to buy moulds from defunct glass companies that had closed during the Depression.

The L. G. Wright Company was unique in glass making for the simple reason that it had no furnace to make the glass, depending solely upon other companies to produce glass for them from Wright's moulds. In 1938, at the onset of Fenton's production of Opalescent Glass, Si Wright approached Frank L. Fenton to produce a Barber Bottle in the Hobnail pattern in Cranberry glass. That was one of the first items that Fenton produced for Wright—and with a few ironic twists of fate (see story in Hobnail Section in the *Fenton Glass Compendium: 1940-70*) pulled the Fenton Company out of the Depression—setting Si Wright up in business and in a long relationship with Fenton.

Over the next sixty years, Fenton would make glass for L. G. Wright. At times, when Fenton orders were slow, as not to idle their workers and furnaces, many items (primarily Opalescent, Overlays, and Blown ware) were produced for Wright. During this time, both Fenton and Wright exchanged moulds with each other for trial or sample shapes and patterns.

L. G. Wright - Cranberry - Dot & Miter - 12" Basket. Rare is the least that could be said about this piece. The story about this pattern is that both Fenton and L. G. Wright had trouble in having moulds made in the Dot & Miter Pattern due to the complex optic. There was suppose to have been a sample run, usually about one-half turn of items made in this pattern. Due to problems in making of it, most of the items that came out of the mould either were broke or cracked. Needless to say that one-half turn was all that was every made of this pattern. So far, this is the only basket to have surfaced in the Dot & Miter pattern. VALUE: UND. *Courtesy of Audrey and Joe Elsinger.*

L. G. Wright - Cranberry - Dot & Miter - 12" Basket.

L. G. Wright - Cranberry - Dot & Miter - Milk Jug: Another item from a very rare pattern. Three are known at the present. One had been in the L. G. Wright Museum until the closure of that company several years ago. With this one, I was lucky enough to be present during the transaction to the present owner, and I will have to say I have never seen anyone whip out a check book and dash off a check so fast in all my life! VALUE: UND. *Courtesy of Linda and John Flippen.*

L. G. Wright - Cranberry - Dot & Miter - 8" Vase. VALUE: UND.

L. G. Wright - French Opalescent - Dot & Miter - 8" Vase. VALUE: UND. *Courtesy of Linda and John Flippen.*

L. G. Wright - Green Opalescent - Daisy & Fern - Finger Bowl: Very few items were produced by Fenton for L. G. Wright in Green Opalescent. I know of three other items, and they are a Satinized version of this Finger Bowl, and a Rib Optic, and a Eye-Dot Barber Bottle. VALUE: UND.

L. G. Wright - Green Opalescent Satin - Daisy & Fern - Finger Bowl. VALUE: UND. *Courtesy of Alice and James Rose.*

L. G. Wright - Cranberry Opalescent - Seaweed Optic/ Honeycomb Optic - Creamers, circa 1950s: Made as a sample item by Fenton for the L. G. Wright Company, this shape was never put into production, nor was the Seaweed pattern. VALUE: UND.

Opalescent - Blue Opalescent - Daisy & Fern Egg: Obviously a Whimsey item that was purchased at the first L. G. Wright auction and was suppose to have came out of Sy Wright's private collection. VALUE: UND. *Courtesy of Chuck Bingham.*

L. G. Wright – Cranberry Opalescent Decorated - Daisy & Fern Coralene Decorated Water Set: NICE is the only word that can be said about this: Nice as in beautiful and Nice as in RARE!! It's not certain whether L. G. Wright had this set decorated, or someone else did this Coralene decoration on their own and then refired the set. Whatever the case may be, it is truly a marvelous item! VALUE: UND.

L. G. Wright - "Screamin' Yellow" Opalescent - Dot Optic Jug/Honey Comb Lamp/Rib Optic Barber Bottle: At one point, possibly during the late 1950s, L. G. Wright ordered this color; but, for some reason, it was only sampled. The unusual thing about it is that it was sampled on both Fenton moulds (*see* items below) and on L. G. Wright moulds. Due to the brightness of the color, I have dubbed this "Screamin' Yellow" Opalescent. Many others call it Goldenrod Opalescent or Golden Yellow Opalescent. When you see it in person you will know why I refer to it as "Screamin' Yellow." For those of you that are familiar with and collect Hall China Dinnerware, you will remember that this is also a color Hall used for a short time in the 1930s, and was also called Screaming Yellow. All Fenton items in this color were made only as samples and are extremely rare. VALUE: UND.

L. G. Wright - "Screamin' Yellow" Opalescent - Hobnail - Star Crimp Sugar and Creamer, circa late 1950s. VALUE: UND. *Courtesy of Alice and James Rose.*

L. G. Wright - "Screamin' Yellow" Opalescent - Coin Dot - #1353 70 oz. Jug: This proves the fact that many times, when Fenton develops a color for another company such as L. G. Wright, they used their own moulds, along with those of the company that they are making the glass for. It's not known if this Coin Dot Jug is one of a kind or if a short turn of these were made. Whatever the case, it is a rare item. VALUE: UND.

L. G. Wright - "Screamin' Yellow" Opalescent - Hobnail - 3" Vase, circa late 1950s. VALUE: UND.

L. G. Wright - Amberina - Wide Rib Optic - Milk Pitcher: Made as a sample in the 1960s, this piece was found at the Factory, before it's closing, etched in the bottom, is F6710 10/5/ 62 VALUE: UND.

L. G. Wright - Deep Cranberry (Fuchsia?) - Thumbprint Optic - 4" Vase: Made as a sample in the early 1970s, this piece has a distinct Purple cast to the Cranberry. Dated 3/13/72 C11- Core/Core Tested, it was also found at the L. G. Wright factory shortly before its closing.

L. G. Wright - Cranberry - Spiral Optic/Eye Dot/Honeycomb - Mini Shades on Brass Lamps: There are no records to indicate whether L. G. Wright specially ordered these shades from Fenton to sell to another company, to be fitted with the brass lamps, or whether they bought the brass lamps and fitted the shades themselves. What is known is that these little guys are very scarce and desirable! VALUE: UND.

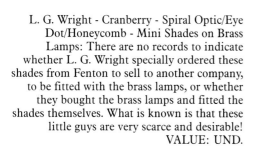

Chapter Nine

1970-1990 Colors/Treatments/Patterns

Burmese - Roses on Burmese - Bell, circa 1970s. It became, in this era of Fenton production, vastly easier to produce one of a kind items, as the decorating department opened in 1968. In the beginning days of the decorating department, many items appeared in hand painted patterns that never were actually put into production. Her talent, and the fact that she was head of the decorating department made Louise Piper the most sought after name among the decorators. In a future volume, I will attempt to cover more of the special items that Louise Piper and many other Fenton decorators created. The bell pictured here is a example of a shape in a regular Fenton pattern that was never put into the Roses on Burmese line. VALUE: $80-$100. *Courtesy of Eileen and Dale Robinson.*

Burmese - Roses on Burmese - 7" Bowl: A unique item that was not in the regular Roses on Burmese line. It was possibly a sample item. On an interesting side note, prior to the completion of the 2001 remodeling of the Fenton Gift Shop at the Fenton factory, there was a special counter set up solely for sample items and whimseys. It was located at the back of the Gift Shop, on the left side of the building. Although it was not labeled as such, many collectors that were in the "know" were aware of it and hit that counter religiously for the off beat items that Fenton had produced recently. Now, since the opening of the remodeled Gift Shop, it is located directly to the left of the main door, just past the retired items counters. VALUE: UND. *Courtesy of Trudy and Dick Green.*

Burmese - Looped Handled 7" Basket, circa 1970s. VALUE: $90-$100. *Courtesy of Lori and Michael Palmer.*

Burmese - Pink Dogwood on Burmese - #7252 7" Vase/#7461 Creamer: Sample items produced prior to Fenton's run of Pink Dogwood on Burmese. VALUE: UND. *Courtesy of Paula and Kevin Parker.*

Burmese - Pink Dogwood on Burmese - 11" Vase/8" Vase: Sample items produced prior to Fenton's run of Pink Dogwood on Burmese. VALUE: UND. *Courtesy of Sharen and Al Creery.*

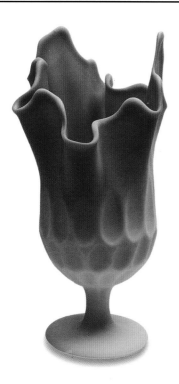

Burmese - Blue Burmese - Pelaton - Creamer & Sugar: Originally this treatment was made by Fenton as a one time issue for the FAGCA, in the early 1980s, as a series of Vases. This creamer and sugar set was made at tha time, also, either as a Whimsey or a sample item. VALUE: UND. *Courtesy o, Trudy and Dick Green.*

Burmese - Thumbprint - Swung Handkerchief Vase: In the 1980s, Government restrictions forced Fenton to stop the production of Burmese for a short while, until new formula could be produced. While this new formula was in development, the id developed to use pressed moulds in Burmese. While experimenting with the pressed moulds, many different pressed moulds were used, resulting in many sample and experimental pieces. It seemed, at the time, that the Thumbprint pattern was one of the favorite patterns to be used, as I have seen quite a few piece of Pressed Burmese this pattern. This is one of the more beautiful examples. VALUE: UND. *Courtesy of Linda and John Flippen.*

Burmese - Blue Burmese - Corn Shock Vase/Basket: Keep in mind that all the items from 1984 in Blue Burmese were never put into the regular Fenton line, except for the Ogee Candy that was in the Connoisseur line. So, any Blue Burmese from that time period could be considered a sample piece. Items in Blue Burmese were sold at the Gift Shop throughout the 1980s. In fact, in 1991, during my first visit to the Fenton Gift Shop, I found several items in Blue Burmese hiding on the lower shelves that had been overlooked by other collectors! VALUE: UND. *Courtesy of Vickie Ticen.*

Burmese - Peachalene - #5150 Alantis Vase: This item was made for Singleton Bailey and was originally intended to have been turned out as glossy regular Burmese. Due to difficulties in making this treatment in this shape, it came out in this color, which Mr. Bailey refused, and which was later sold in the Fenton Gift Shop. It is now considered Peachalene and is highly collectible due to the very limited issue. VALUE: UND. *Courtesy of Trudy and Dick Green.*

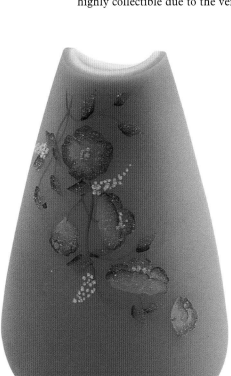

Rose Quartz - Morning Glories on Rose Quartz - 6" Vase: In the early 1980s, prior to Fenton's introduction of Rose Quartz in the Connoisseur line, there must have been quite a few sample runs of this color. Keep in mind that this is the first time that this color was ever offered, and it had been derived from the formula that would become Blue Burmese. It is not known whether this vase was painted at the time of production or later on. It is interesting to note that, when Rose Quartz was put into production, it was not hand decorated but sand blasted. VALUE: UND. *Courtesy of Chuck Bingham.*

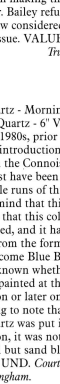

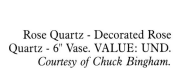

Rose Quartz - Decorated Rose Quartz - 6" Vase. VALUE: UND. *Courtesy of Chuck Bingham.*

151

Rosalene - Wild Strawberry Whimsey Toothpick: Originally made for the FAGCA in Satin Rosalene, this little item was produced at the same time in Glossy, with an iridized Finish and a strange cupped crimped top. VALUE: UND. *Courtesy of Trudy and Dick Green.*

Roselene – Waterlily Oval Comport/Plumes Cologne Bottle: Two Sample items produced in Rosalene, the Oval Comport possible produced prior to 1976, when they were attempting to prefect the Roselene treatment. VALUE: UND. *Courtesy of Trudy and Dick Green.*

Rosalene - Butterfly in Net - Creamer/Basket/Mug: POP QUIZ: Which of these three items was the regular issue? If you answered the Mug, you are correct. This mug was made in the 1980s for the FAGCA as a souvenir for one of the Fenton Conventions. The Basket and Creamer were Whimsey items made at the same time. VALUE: UND. *Courtesy of Trudy and Dick Green.*

Roselene - Logo/#3480 Cactus Cookie Jar: Two unique items, the cookie jar was possibly a sample produced during the time that Fenton was perfecting the Rosalene process. VALUE: UND. *Courtesy of Dick and Trudy Green.*

Roselane - Basket Weave Jug, circa late 1980s. VALUE: UND. *Courtesy of Noralee and Ralph Rogers.*

Favrene - #5171 Butterfly on Stand/Logo: Two sample items that Fenton produced when sampling this treatment, prior to its first introduction in the late 1980s. VALUE: UND. *Courtesy of Dick and Trudy Green.*

Favrene - Snowman Vase/Butterfly Vase/Ginger Jar: It sometimes makes a person wonder why, of all the treatments that Fenton produced, the most beautiful and awe-inspiring are also the most difficult and expensive to manufacture!! That was the case with Favrene. When first introduced in the late 1980s, it was regulated to Club Souvenirs and the Connoisseur line because of the price and difficulty of production. These items were made as Sample items for the 1994 Connoisseur line. VALUE: UND. *Courtesy of Trudy and Dick Green.*

Favrene - Freehand Vases: Although the 1976 Robert Barber freehand items were not a commercial success, Fenton still (when in the process of developing a new treatment) cannot resist the temptation to produce a few freehand items from it (Thank God for that!!). These Faverene freehand items were made in the late 1980s. VALUE: UND. *Courtesy of Trudy and Dick Green.*

Favrene - Hobnail - #3752 11" Vase: Keep in mind that many hours went into recreating this beautiful Tiffany treatment. Even today, it is the most sought after of Fenton's achievements of the past fifty years. VALUE: UND. *Courtesy of Sharon and Al Creery.*

Favrene - Deco Lady Figural: Although not marked with a Fenton logo, this item is suppose to be Fenton. According to the owner, it was both a sample item on a sample mould that was made during the early 1990s run of Faverene. It was suppose to have been carried out in a lunch box (so to speak) and is now in a private collection. It is not known whether there are any others from this run. VALUE: UND.

Favrene - Deco Lady Figural: Back side of Figure.

Carnival - Original Formula (Amethyst) - Hobnail Hand Vase, circa 1970s: Made as a sample item. VALUE: $100-$125. *Courtesy of Lori and Michael Palmer.*

Carnival - Ruby #9480 Chessie Candy Box. VALUE: $200-$250. *Courtesy of Trudy and Dick Green.*

Carnival - Ruby - Holly Basket. VALUE: $70-$100. *Courtesy of Trudy and Dick Green.*

Carnival - Ruby - #8489 Lily of the Valley - Candy Box.
VALUE: $100-$150. *Courtesy of Adonna and Elmer Pusker.*

Carnival - Orange - Strawberry
Salt and Pepper Shakers, circa
1970s. VALUE: UND. *Courtesy
of Lori and Michael Palmer.*

Carnival - White Carnival - #9480
Chessie Candy Box: Produced in
the 1980s off of a very collectible
and desirable mould. VALUE:
$150-$200. *Courtesy of Trudy and
Dick Green.*

Stretch - Velva Rose - Persian Medallion - Chalice: As the
1960s and 1970s progressed, it seemed that fewer actually
Whimsey items appeared. This Chalice, with the cupped
and crimped edge, is one of the few that has surfaced.
VALUE: UND. *Courtesy of Susie, Tiffany, and Ron Ballard.*

Carnival - Ruby - Hobnail - #3761/#3843 Wine Set: Fenton achieved great
success in the 1970s with the reintroduction of their famous Carnival Glass.
Many items which were never in the regular Carnival line were sprayed with
the iridescent spray. The most impressive of these was the Ruby Hobnail Wine
Set. VALUE: Decanter: $300-$400; Goblets: $50-$70 each. *Courtesy of Audrey
and Joe Elsinger.*

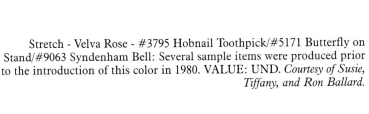

Stretch - Velva Rose - #3795 Hobnail Toothpick/#5171 Butterfly on
Stand/#9063 Syndenham Bell: Several sample items were produced prior
to the introduction of this color in 1980. VALUE: UND. *Courtesy of Susie,
Tiffany, and Ron Ballard.*

Crest - Blue Ridge - 1 Pc. Fairy Light: Made as a sample item during the production of the 1985 anniversary issue of Blue Ridge. VALUE: UND. *Courtesy of Alice and James Rose.*

Crest - Hobnail with Cobalt Crest - Heart Relish, circa mid-1980s: A very unusual item topped off with pink handle, possibly made for sale in the Gift Shop. VALUE: UND. *Courtesy of Darcie Smith.*

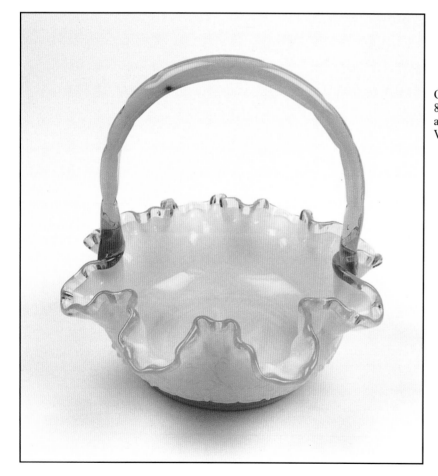

Crest - Gold Crest on Custard - Spanish Lace - #3539 8.5" Basket: A very unusual treatment, possibly made as a trial run to be considered for later production. VALUE: UND. *Courtesy of Williamstown Antique Mall.*

Crest - Ruby Snow Crest - #7237 7" Basket: Possibly made at the same time as the Ruby Snow Crest Heart Relish, which was produced for Valentine's Day in the early 1980s. VALUE: $150-$200. *Courtesy of Jan Hollingsworth.*

Crest - Ruby Snow Crest - 7" Basket. VALUE: $150-$200. *Courtesy of Jan Hollingsworth.*

Decorated Milk Glass - Roses on Hobnail - #3886 Hobnail Candy/#7451 Silver Crest Vase: Although the candy was in the regular Roses on Hobnail line, it is a very scarce item. The Silver Crest Vase was not in the line. VALUE: Candy: $100-$125; Silver Crest Vase: UND. *Courtesy of Eileen and Dale Robinson.*

Decorated Milk Glass - Blue Bells on Hobnail - Eggs/#7357 Silver Crest Fan Vase/ #7333 Silver Crest Heart Relish/#5165 Cat: These items are sure to make any Blue Bells collector break out into a cold sweat. Note the variations of the decorations on the eggs. The other three items were never in actual production. VALUE: UND. *Courtesy of Eileen and Dale Robinson.*

Decorated Milk Glass - Pink Flowers on Silver Crest - #1923 7" Top Hat, circa 1970s. VALUE: UND. *Courtesy of Eileen and Dale Robinson.*

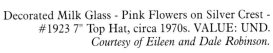

Decorated Milk Glass - Pink Flowers on Hobnail - #3802 Margarine Tub: A decoration that was sampled but never brought into production. VALUE: UND. *Courtesy of Wanell and Walt Jones.*

Decorated Milk Glass - Violets in the Snow - #1920 12" Top Hat, circa 1970s. VALUE: UND. *Courtesy of Jessie and Bill Ramsey.*

Decorated Milk Glass - #9254 Rose Milk Glass with Pink Roses - Handkerchief Vase: Made for Sears in the early 1970s as a sample to consider at the same time they were to produce the Rose Milk Glass with Talisman Roses. VALUE: UND. *Courtesy of Laurie and Rich Karman.*

Decorated Milk Glass - #9235 Rose Milk Glass with Blue Roses - 10" Basket: Sometimes it makes you wonder why the items sampled were not put into the line, rather than the items chosen! This basket was found in a small antique shop in Williamstown West Virginia, so it never strayed far from home. VALUE: UND. *Courtesy of Sue Gomer.*

Decorated Milk Glass - Milk Glass with Blue Wash - #8233 Cherries Bowl: Made for a very short time in this treatment in the early 1970s. It was also made at the same time in a yellow/green wash. VALUE: $50-$60.

Opalescent - Blue Opalescent - 299 Owl Ring Tree: A sample em, possibly produced in the late 1980s at the time that Fenton reintroduced Blue Opalescent into the line. VALUE: UND. *Author's Collection.*

palescent - Blue Opalescent -

Opalescent - Blue Opalescent - Sculptured Ice Optic – Pitcher, 1983. VALUE: UND. *Courtesy of Emogene Snyder.*

Opalescent - Cranberry - Baby Coin Dot or Honeycomb- Ring Neck Bottle/Vase. VALUE: UND. *Courtesy of Linda and John Flippen.*

Opalescent - Cranberry - Baby Coin Dot or Honeycomb- Cruet. VALUE: $150-$200. *Courtesy of John & Linda Flippen.*

Opalescent - Cranberry Satin - Baby Coin Dot or Honeycomb - Whimsey Ring Neck Vase. VALUE: UND. *Courtesy of Trudy and Dick Green.*

Opalescent - Cranberry - Coin Dot Cruet:
Made in the mid-1980s. VALUE: $200-$250.
Courtesy of Betty and Ike Hardman.

Opalescent - Cranberry - Baby Coin Dot or Honeycomb -
11" Jack in the Pulpit Vase with Ruby Crest, circa 1991
VALUE: UND.

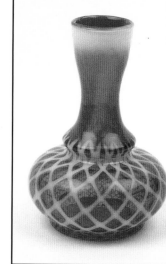

Opalescent - Cranberry - Coin Dot - Fairy
Light 2 pc.: Made in the 1980s. VALUE:
$150-$200. *Courtesy of Linda and John
Flippen.*

Opalescent - Cranberry - Diamond
Optic - Vase: Made in the 1980s.
VALUE: $125-$150. *Courtesy of Janice
and Gordy Bowerman.*

Opalescent - Cranberry - Daisy Optic - 7"
Basket: This basket, and others in differe[nt]
optics, plus several vase and rose bowl
shapes, were made in 1978 for the FAGCA
second convention, to show the process of
making glass from optic moulds. The secr[et]
to telling these baskets from the ones that
were made as samples on into the 1980s a[nd]
1990s (as these baskets carry the Fenton
Logo) is to observe the handle. This is the
old Bamboo handle that was used in the
1940s-60s. The later handle has Opal in it
and is usually twisted into an optic effect [or]
ribbed. VALUE: UND. *Courtesy of Linda a[nd]
John Flippen.*

Opalescent - Cranberry - Coin Dot -
6" Vase. VALUE: $125-$150.
Courtesy of John and Linda Flippen.

Opalescent - Cranberry - Double Wedding Ring - Rose Bowl, circa late 1980s. VALUE: UND. *Courtesy of Betty and Ike Hardman.*

Opalescent - Cranberry - Dot Optic - 10" Vase/4" Vase, circa late 1980s. VALUE: UND. *Courtesy of Linda and John Flippen.*

Opalescent - Cranberry - Double Wedding Ring - Rose Bowl, circa late 1980s: Notice the different opening in this one compared to the previous rose bowl. VALUE: UND. *Courtesy of Janice and Gordy Bowerman.*

Opalescent - Cranberry - Daisy & Fern - Feather Optic - Cruets: Made in the mid-1980s as Sample items. VALUE: $175-$200. *Courtesy of Trudy and Dick Green.*

Opalescent - Cranberry - Fern
Optic – Cruet, 1972 (pre-Logo):
Made as a sample. VALUE: UND.

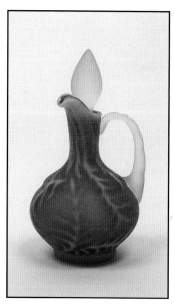

Opalescent- Cranberry - Feather Optic - Looped
Handled Basket: Made in the mid-1980s as a sample
item. VALUE: $125-$150. *Courtesy of Trudy and Dick
Green.*

Opalescent - Cranberry - Fern Optic/Honeycomb Optic -
Ewer/Cruet: Ewer, circa 1978; Cruet, circa 1972: Both
items were made as samples. VALUE: UND.

Opalescent - Cranberry - Rib Optic/Heart
- Rose Bowls. VALUE: $100-$125.
Courtesy of Trudy and Dick Green.

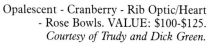

Opalescent - Cranberry -
Unknown Optic – Cruet.
VALUE: $150-$175.

Opalescent - Cranberry - Rib Optic/Snowflake
Optic Baskets. VALUE: $175-$200. *Courtesy of
Trudy and Dick Green.*

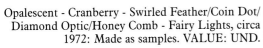

Opalescent - Cranberry - Swirled Feather/Coin Dot/
Diamond Optic/Honey Comb - Fairy Lights, circa
1972: Made as samples. VALUE: UND.

Opalescent - Cranberry -
Heart Optic/Drape Optic/
Wide Rib Optic - Fairy
Light/Baskets. VALUE:
Fairy Lights: $350+;
Basket $175-$200. *Courtesy
of Alice and James Rose.*

Opalescent - Cranberry - Coindot/ Dot Optic/Diamond Optic -Fairy Light: In 1983 a limited series of these one piece Fairy Lights were produced for the FAGCA Club during their convention in Parkersburg, West Virginia. They were made to demonstrate the way optic moulds were used to make Opalescent Glass. Now very scarce and very desirable, they cause a stir whenever one appears on the market. Notice the difference in the crimp on the two Dot Optic lights. The next few pictures will show the wide variety of Optics employed for this occasion. VALUE: $350 each. *Courtesy of Emogene Snyder.*

Opalescent - Cranberry – Sculptured Ice Optic/Diamond Optic/Dot Optic Zipper Optic - 1 Pc. Fairy Lights. VALUE: $350+. *Courtesy of Emogene Snyder.*

Opalescent - Cranberry - Honeycomb Optic - 1 Pc. Fairy Light. VALUE: $350+.

Opalescent - Cranberry - Unknown Optic - 1 Pc. Fairy Light. VALUE: $350+.

Opalescent - Cranberry - Spiral Optic - 1 Pc. Fairy Light. VALUE: $350+. *Courtesy of Linda and John Flippen.*

Opalescent - Cranberry - 1 Pc. Fairy Light. VALUE: $350+. *Courtesy of Jan Hollingsworth.*

Opalescent - French Opalescent - #8251 Mandarin/#8252 Empress Vases: After Fenton bought the Verley's moulds in 1966 from Holophane Lighting company, these two vases were issued in Colonial Orange and French Opalescent. Neither of these color are easy to locate. Possibly the French Opalescent is more scarce and more desirable. VALUE: $75-$100 each.

Opalescent - Decorated French Opalescent - Strawberries on French Opalescent - Sample Student Lamp, circa 1983: Notice the inventive way the top to the Fairy Light was put to use in the sample lamp. The regular Lamp did not have any glass in the lamp base. VALUE: UND. *Courtesy of Claire and Allan Kauffung.*

Opalescent - Plum Opalescent - Mini Hand Vases: According to Carolyn Grable, who these were made for, there were only three of these made, as the moulds were switched shortly before the production of her Kissing Kids in Plum Opalescent, and it was not realized until these vases had already been produced. Although made in the late 1990s, these Mini Hand Vases very desirable and unusual. VALUE: UND. *Courtesy of Carolyn and Dick Grable.*

Opaque - Barely Blue - Wheat Vase: This usual item was never marketed in Barely Blue Satin, let alone in Glossy Barely Blue. This is a real unusual find for the Wheat Vase collector! VALUE: UND. *Courtesy of Vickie Ticen.*

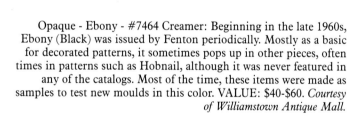

Opaque - Ebony - #7464 Creamer: Beginning in the late 1960s, Ebony (Black) was issued by Fenton periodically. Mostly as a basic for decorated patterns, it sometimes pops up in other pieces, often times in patterns such as Hobnail, although it was never featured in any of the catalogs. Most of the time, these items were made as samples to test new moulds in this color. VALUE: $40-$60. *Courtesy of Williamstown Antique Mall.*

Opaque - Cameo - Rose Candy Bottom: I know that this item was meant to have been satinized later on, but is makes for an usual piece. It also makes you wonder what the whole Rose line would of looked like in Cameo Satin. VALUE: UND.

Opaque - Custard #1353 8" Vase: A very unusual item as this mould had been out of circulation for some years when this item was made and, also, as it was done in a glossy finish instead of the regular satin finish. VALUE: UND. *Courtesy of Trudy and Dick Green.*

Opaque - Milk Glass Iridized - Peacock Vase, circa 1980s. VALUE: $80-$100. *Courtesy of Noralee and Ralph Rogers.*

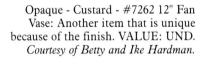

Opaque - Custard - #7262 12" Fan Vase: Another item that is unique because of the finish. VALUE: UND. *Courtesy of Betty and Ike Hardman.*

Opaque - Mandarin Red - Hobnail - #3992 Top Hat: Made as a sample sometime in the late 1960s, prior to the time that Fenton started to put logos on their items. Various treatments from the 1920s were sampled at this time, including Mongolian Green and Pekin Blue; but, due to difficulties in both achieving the colors and the manufacturing process involved in these treatments, they were never put into production. VALUE: UND. *Courtesy of Eileen and Dale Robinson.*

Opaque - Mandarin Red - Hobnail - Candle Bowl. VALUE: UND. *Courtesy of Sharen and Al Creery.*

Opaque - Mongolian Green - Verlys Planters, circa 1960s. Possibly produced at the same time that the Jonquil Yellow and Pekin Blue items were produced in 1969, and never put in productions because of the difficulty of the process necessary to produce the color. VALUE: UND. *Courtesy of Eileen and Dale Robinson.*

Opaque - Patriot Red - Jefferson Covered Bowl, 1976: Made as a sample during the production of the Bicentennial items, prior to 1976. VALUE: UND. *Courtesy of Williamstown Mall.*

Opaque - Pekin Blue - Beaded Melon Dresser Set, circa late 1960s. From the number of items that appeared in this line (keeping in mind that it was never put into regular production, and all items in this color and Jonquil Yellow are considered sample items), you can get a sense for just how many things might be in circulation in other items, colors, and patterns; products made over the years as Sample items. VALUE: UND. *Courtesy of Betty and Ike Hardman.*

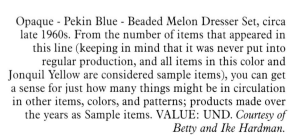

Opaque - Ruby Slag - Tall Candlesticks/Mini Basket/Flower Pot: It is uncertain whether these items were made during the run of Ruby Slag for Levay or whether they were produce some time later. Notice the use of the Flower Pot mould that had been purchased from AKRO AGATE, which later was used to make Jadeite Flower Pots for Martha Stewart. VALUE: UND. *Courtesy of Trudy and Dick Green.*

Opaque - Purple Slag with Snow Crest - #5858 Wheat Vase, circa mid-1980s. VALUE: UND. *Courtesy of Vickie Ticen.*

Opaque - Ruby Slag - Leaf Votive, 1980s. VALUE: UND. *Courtesy of Phil Barber.*

Opaque - Iridized Shell Pink - Shell Vase: A unique item made off of an old Cambridge mould in the late 1980s. VALUE: UND. *Courtesy of Trudy and Dick Green.*

Opaque - Various Colors - Hobnail - Ashtray/Footed Ivy Ball/Handled Bonbon/Mini Mug: There are some days that can be classified as bad days at the glass factory. I would say that, from the way that these unique colors look, the day these were made was one of them. These items were made in the late 1960s or early 1970s. VALUE: UND. *Courtesy of the Williamstown Antique Mall.*

Opaque - Various Colors - Hobnail - Mini Candle Bowl. VALUE: UND. *Courtesy of Phil Barber.*

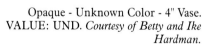

Opaque - Unknown Color - 4" Vase. VALUE: UND. *Courtesy of Betty and Ike Hardman.*

Opaque - Unknown Color/Treatment - #5858 Wheat Vase. VALUE: UND. *Courtesy of Vickie Ticen.*

Overlay - Milk Glass with Spangles - Hobnail - #3728 Comport/#3753 Footed Swung Vase: Made very much in the same way as Vasa Murrhina is produced. If these were sample items, it would be been interesting to see a complete line. VALUE: UND. *Courtesy of Eileen and Dale Robinson.*

Overlay – Amethyst Overlay - #8429 Waterlily Rose Bowl. VALUE: $60-$80. *Courtesy of Eileen and Dale Robinson.*

Overlay - Decorated Candleglow Yellow -#2050 7" Vase: It sometimes has puzzled me that, when Fenton has produced a line of certain treatments such as the Overlay colors from the 1980s, they don't experiment with them more than what they do. I for one like the idea of the decorated Overlay, like the item illustrated here. Keep in mind, in a little over ten years since this piece was produced, that Fenton decorated several Overlay colors and sold them in their regular line. VALUE: $80-$100. *Courtesy of Trudy and Dick Green.*

Overlay - Candle Glow Yellow - Corn Shock Vase, circa 1984. VALUE: UND. *Courtesy of Vickie Ticen.*

171

Overlay - Forget Me
Knot Blue - Bubble
Optic - Basket.
VALUE: $100-$125.

Overlay - Dusty Rose Overlay with Peach Blow
Interior - Caprice Basket, circa 1987: This treatment
was made for the FAGCA in 1987. This piece was one
of the Whimsey items that was auctioned off during
the convention banquet. VALUE: UND. *Courtesy of
Noralee and Ralph Rogers.*

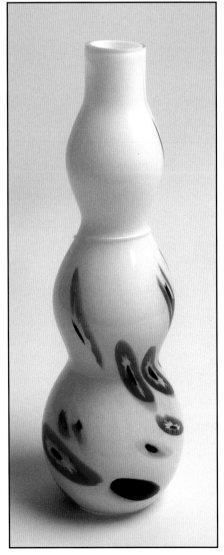

Overlay - Decorated Heritage
Green - #1866 Creamer.
VALUE: $80-$100. *Courtesy of
Trudy and Dick Green.*

Overlay - Milk Glass with Millefiori - New World Wine Bottle: You can
almost always count on the fact that, when Fenton experiments with a
completely new treatment, it seems to pop up on a desirable mould from a
previous treatment! VALUE: UND. *Courtesy of Sharen and Al Creery.*

Overlay - Pink Over Milk Glass with Silver Flecks - #7451 Vase, early 1980s: A unique treatment in which Pink Glass was gathered over Milk Glass. VALUE: UND. *Courtesy of Chuck Bingham.*

Overlay - Opaque Blue - #8464 Water Lily Jug: A very good example of a color that had been discontinued some years earlier appearing on a newer mould. In this case, the Opaque Blue color had been discontinued for a good ten years before Fenton started to use this shape. VALUE: UND. *Courtesy of Betty and Ike Hardman.*

Overlay - Pink Over Milk Glass with Silver Flecks – Vase, early 1980s. VALUE: UND. *Courtesy of Betty and Ike Hardman.*

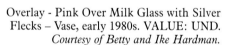

Overlay - Plated Amberina - Basket/11" Vase/Cane: Notice the unique looped handle on the Basket. These items were produced during the 1963 run of Plated Amberina, except for the Cane, which was in the Connoisseur line in 1983. VALUE: Basket-11" Vase: UND; Cane: $150-$250. *Courtesy of Trudy and Dick Green.*

Overlay - Plated Amberina - #5858 Jack in the Pulpit Wheat Vase, circa mid-1980s: A very unusual item, first off, as the Plated Amberina color is on the inside, and then it's finished off with a Jack in the Pulpit Crimp to boot. VALUE: UND. *Courtesy of Vickie Ticen.*

Overlay - Plated Amberina Iridized - 11" Vase: Made in the 1970s as a sample treatment. VALUE: UND.

Overlay - Unknown Colors - Hobnail - #3752 11" Vases: There must have been some minds working overtime to create these Overlay colors that came out of the 1970s. These colors also appear in the 10" Crest Bowls. VALUE: UND. *Courtesy of Sharen Creery.*

Overlay - Unknown Colors - Hobnail - #3830 10" Bowl. VALUE: UND. *Courtesy of Connie and Aaron Patient.*

Overlay - Rose Vasa Murrhina - Vase/Rose Bowl, early 1980s. VALUE: UND. *Courtesy of Chuck Bingham.*

Overlay - Vasa Murrhina - Cruet, circa 1983: Notice the Cruet to the left with the clear handle and stopper. This one was a sample. When this piece reached the Connoisseur line, it was decided to go with the Satin Handle and Stopper. VALUE: UND. *Courtesy of Lori and Michael Palmer.*

Overlay - Vasa Murrhina - #9055 Ribbed Vase: This shape was made as a sample to go with the Vasa Murrhina Connoisseur items made in 1983. VALUE: UND.

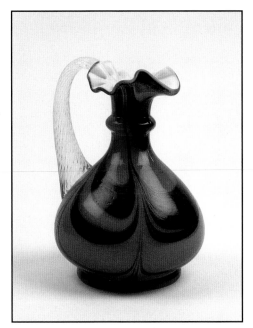

Overlay - Wild Rose Overlay with Deep Purple Swirls - Cruet: Another treatment that amazes me, which was never put into production, either because of the time and cost involved in making it, or from difficulties in producing it. VALUE: UND. *Courtesy of Eileen and Dale Robinson.*

175

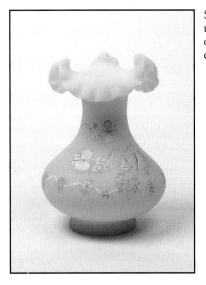

Satin - Blue Satin - Decorated Butterflies - #7252 Vase: Look closely and see if you can spot the very unusual aspect of this item. It's actually the same pattern as Butterflies on Milk Glass, but this time it's on Barely Blue Satin. This is probably a sample item, dating from when this pattern was being considered for production. VALUE: UND. *Courtesy of Dick and Carolyn Grable.*

Satin - Blue Satin - Hobnail - Candle Bowl/Comport/Planter/Vase: These items are unique in the sense that they were never originally issued in Blue Satin, but in the Glossy Blue Satin that Fenton called Blue Glow, and because they were only issued for a short time in 1980. To find any of these in Blue Satin is to find a real treasure! VALUE: Candle Bowl: $70-$100; Comport: $60-$80; Planter: $60-$80; Vase: $60-$80. *Courtesy of Susie, Tiffany, and Ron Ballard.*

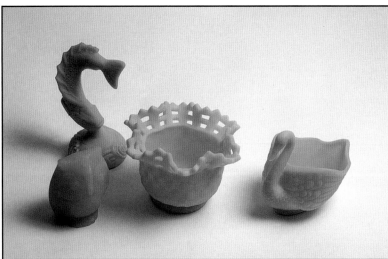

Satin - Blue Satin - #5186 Owl/#5193 Dolphin on Stand/#8222 Basket Weave Bowl/Open Swan: Unique items that were not in the regular Blue Satin line. VALUE: UND. *Courtesy of Susie, Tiffany, and Ron Ballard.*

SATIN - Blue Satin - #6056 Wave Crest Vase/6.5" Vase/#8428 Scroll & Eye Comport/#8427 Pinwheel Oval Comport: Four more items that were not in the regular Blue Satin line, but shapes that appeared in other Fenton Lines during the 1970s. VALUE: UND. *Courtesy of Susie, Tiffany, and Ron Ballard.*

Satin - Custard Satin - #3733 Hobnail Heart Relish: A sample item made in the 1970s. Very few items in Hobnail made it into the Satin Line at that time. It's amazing that this one didn't, due to the popularity of this shape now. It just goes to show how tastes change over a few decades. VALUE: UND. *Courtesy of Sharon and Al Creery.*

Satin - Custard Satin - Pink Blossom - Heart Relish: As I always like to say, "Put this one on eBay and watch the phone lines melt down." This is a very desirable item in a very desirable pattern. It was made as a sample item in the mid-1970s. VALUE: UND. *Courtesy of Laurie and Richard Karman.*

Satin - Decorated Custard Satin - #7251 11" Vase with Scene: A unique item with a decoration that I personally wished would have made it to the Fenton line! Notice the shading used at the top of the vase to make it look like Burmese. VALUE: UND. *Courtesy of Sharen and Al Creery.*

Satin - White Satin - Decorated Chessie Box: A very realistic sample item with a delicate blue wash. Now to find the lid for it!!! VALUE: UND. *Courtesy of Betty and Ike Hardman.*

Transparent - Colonial Blue - Mini Hand Vase, 1960s?: It's very uncommon for a mould at Fenton that has been in retirement for over twenty years to be drawn out of the vault and used only for a sample item; but, it looks like that was the case in this instance. This mould was used in the early 1940s and was used on a limited basis in the 1980s and 1990s. VALUE: UND. *Courtesy of the Kansas City Fenton Finders Club.*

Transparent - Hobnail - Colonial Pink - #3733 Heart Relish: Keep in mind that the only thing offered in the regular Fenton line in Colonial Pink, in the Hobnail pattern, is the Slipper. To find a sample item such as this, in this color, is a real prize. VALUE: UND. *Courtesy of Jan Hollingsworth.*

Transparent - Hobnail - ORANGE - 8" Low Basket: A unique item made off the 8" Bonbon Mould for a sample, circa 1965. VALUE: $50-$70.

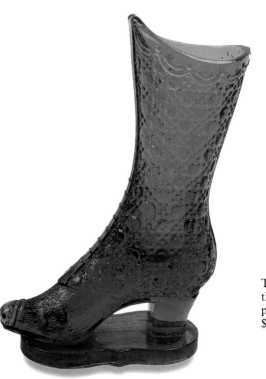

Transparent - Colonial Blue - Boot: Not many people are aware that this boot appeared in the Fenton catalog, circa 1966. Only produced for one year, it seldom appears on the market. VALUE: $40-$60. *Courtesy of Eileen and Dale Robinson.*

Transparent - Hobnail - Ruby - Large Shaker: Made in the mid-1960s as a sample item. VALUE: UND. *Courtesy of Millie Coty.*

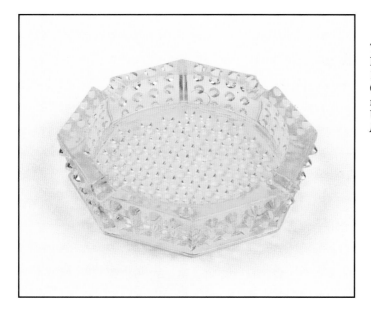

Transparent - Hobnail - Topaz - Large Hexagonal Ashtray: Made in the early 1980s at the same time that Topaz Opalescent was in production, but made without the Opal. VALUE: UND. *Courtesy of Betty and Ike Hardman.*

Transparent - Hobnail - Teal Green? - 4.5" Footed Vase: Possibly made as part of the OVG Line. VALUE: $25-$30. *Courtesy of Millie Coty.*

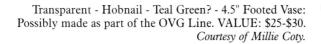

Transparent - Rose - Colonial Pink - #9206 Shakers: Made as sample items in the mid-1960s. These were never in the regular Rose line, but were made regularly in Milk Glass and in the other Colonial colors of Blue, Amber, and Green. VALUE: UND. *Author's Collection.*

Transparent - Rose - Topaz - #9222 Comport: A unique item in an unusual color that was made as a sample in the early 1980s. VALUE: UND. *Courtesy of Williamstown Mall.*

Transparent - Thumbprint - Colonial Blue - 4466 Fat Pitcher: A unique item made for only one year in 1968. (Also see this shape in Colonial Green, which follows.) VALUE: $150-$200. *Courtesy of Elizabeth Hendrix.*

Transparent - Thumbprint - Colonial Blue - 12" Bowl/Small Comport: Made as Whimsey items, the bowl is off the mould of the Fat Pitcher pictured previously. Notice the spot toward the back of the bowl, close to the base, where the handle was to be applied. The comport was made off the mould for the top of the Chip 'n' Dip. VALUE: UND. *Courtesy of Elizabeth Hendrix.*

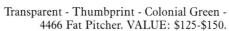

Transparent - Thumbprint - Colonial Green - 4466 Fat Pitcher. VALUE: $125-$150.

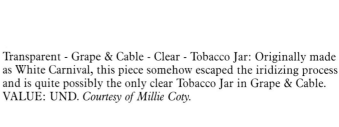

Transparent - Grape & Cable - Clear - Tobacco Jar: Originally made as White Carnival, this piece somehow escaped the iridizing process and is quite possibly the only clear Tobacco Jar in Grape & Cable. VALUE: UND. *Courtesy of Millie Coty.*

Chapter Ten

1970-1990 Special Series Items (Robert Barber)

Robert Barber Prototype Items

Robert Barber was a glass maker who had been employed earlier by Fenton, when his glass furnace had burned the building down it was housed in during an attempt to create off hand ware reminiscent of the items produced by Fenton in the 1920s. Throughout a six week period in 1975, the free hand prototype items shown below were designed by Robert Barber and produced by a young Dave Fetty and Delmar Stowasser. Fetty and Stowasser later on would become famous in their own right in Fenton art glass circles for the Artisan line that Delmar Stowasser produced in the 1980s and the off hand ware that has been made by Dave Fetty throughout his tenure at Fenton.

Robert Barber - 8.5" Feather Vase: The Feather Vase is unique, with deep Amethyst Feathers cascading down the sides. VALUE: $500+. *Courtesy of Clair and Kauffung.*

Robert Barber - Feather Bottle/8" Vase: The Feather Bottle was made in the same way that the Feather Vases were produced, by taking an ice pick to the hot glass and pulling it down to form the pattern. David Fetty has confirmed that he was the person who made the bottle, and it was the only one made. The Turquoise and Black 8" Vase is supposed to be one of a kind, and originally sold at an FAGCA Convention as a raffle item. VALUE: Bottle: $1,000 +; Vase: $750+ (Please keep in mind on the prices on these sample Robert Barber items, that they are the opinion of the owner, arrived at by combining her observations of similar items when they appeared for sale on the open market with what she feels they should be worth.). *Courtesy of Claire and Alan Kauffung.*

Robert Barber - Cascade Pitcher: The more you see of these items, the more beautiful they become. Keep in mind that these pieces were made by a talented group of glassmakers in a sixty day period. Most are signed with the Fenton logo, plus the year 1976 etched on each item. The Cascade Pitcher is 7" tall and 7.5" in diameter and was made off the regular production Cascade Vase by Delmar Stowasser. I keep telling the owner of this item that this is the one I want! She won't even talk to me about it!! VALUE: $1,500+. *Courtesy of Claire and Alan Kauffung.*

Robert Barber - 10.5" Jack in the Pulpit Vase/16" Two Branch Vase/7" Mandarin Red Type Vase: Three unique items, in colors that were completely uncommon in the regular Robert Barber line made for Fenton. Dave Fetty confirmed that the twin branch vase was made by both Robert Barber and himself. Many people confuse the Orange and Black Vase for an original Fenton Karnak Vase from the 1920s, done in Mandarin Red. VALUE: 10" Jack in the Pulpit Vase: $500+; Two Branch Vase: $1,500+; Mandarin Red Vase: $500+. *Courtesy of Claire and Alan Kauffung.*

Robert Barber Items - 9" Pitcher Vase/8.5" Cobalt Doughnut Vase/9.5" Blue Doughnut Vase: The way these items are formed has to boggle the imagination of a making glass novice! While hot, the glass worker takes a sharp pick and pierces the side of the vase. He then keeps working on the hole until it extends all the way through the piece, and the inside of the piercing is healed over. The 9" pitcher and light Blue vase are Milk Glass cased with Blue and then Crystal. The Cobalt Doughnut Vase is Milk Glass over Cobalt, then iridized. VALUE: Pitcher Vase: $750+; Doughnut Vases: $500+ each. *Courtesy of Claire and Alan Kauffung.*

Robert Barber Items - 9.5" Cobalt Doughnut Vase. VALUE: UND. *Courtesy of Roserita Ziegler.*

Robert Barber Items - 9" Cobalt Doughnut Vase.
VALUE: $500+. *Courtesy of Claire and Alan Kauffung.*

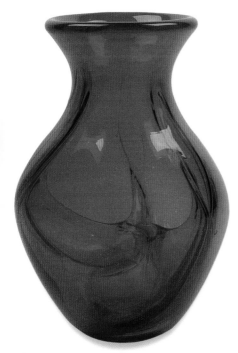

Robert Barber Items - 11" Custard Vase with Tree/9" Favrene Type Vase: According to Dave Fetty, who made the Custard Vase, the glass frit in the vase was laid out on a table to resemble a tree and then, while still hot, the vase was rolled on it. In an interesting note, according to the owner of most of these items, Robert Barber did not produce these items himself. He would design them and decided what treatment and colors they would be made in, and then depended on people like Delmar Stowasser, Dave Fetty, and Bill Sage to do the actual production. The Favrene Vase was one of Fenton's first attempts to recreate the old Tiffany Art Glass treatments. VALUE: Custard Vase with Trees: $750+; Favrene Vase: $500+. *Courtesy of Claire and Alan Kauffung.*

Robert Barber Items - 8" Multichambered Vase: To produce the design in this vase, several different chambers were blown on the inside of this piece. VALUE: $600+. *Courtesy of Claire and Alan Kauffung.*

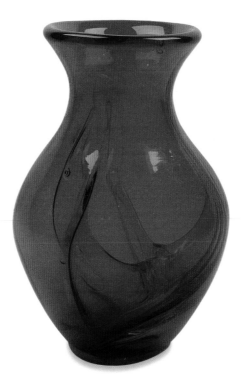

Robert Barber Items - 8" Multichambered Vase. VALUE: $600+. *Courtesy of Claire and Alan Kauffung.*

183

Robert Barber Items - 9.5" Ebony Jug: This piece appears to have the initials "SP" inscribed on the bottom. By doing some research, the owner found out that this was actually "DS," and stood for Fenton glass worker Delmar Stowasser, who had been on the Barber team during the production of these items. The piece is also marked with an "S," which at that time stood for Sample. It was much later, actually in the early 1990s, that the "S" incised on the bottom stood for second. VALUE: $600+. *Courtesy of Claire and Alan Kauffung.*

Robert Barber Items - Turquoise & Yellow Vase/Black Thin Neck Vase: Both of these items were made by Robert Barber, in his studio, before he came to Fenton in 1975. Both pieces are unique and unusual. After his departure from Fenton, in 1977, Robert Barber worked at Pilgrim and later reopened his own studio. VALUE: Turquoise & Yellow Vase: $300+; Black Thin Neck Vase: $250+. *Courtesy of Claire and Alan Kauffung.*

Robert Barber Items - Wild Rose Overlay Doughnut Vase: It's surprising to see, in the midst of all the vibrant colors and hues used in the production of the Barber Art Glass items, that at times Fenton would revert back to an old standard treatment to create one of these items. VALUE: UND. *Courtesy of Eileen and Dale Robinson.*

Robert Barber Items - Footed Vases: On both of these vases the feet were made by literally pulling the glass down while hot to form the feet! The Light Blue with Aventurine Green Frit once belonged to Bill Fenton and was later donated to the National Fenton Glass Society for an auction. It is not only signed Dave Fetty and has the Fenton Logo, but also is signed by Bill Fenton. The ruffle was created by taking a pair of shears and cutting the glass while hot. This treatment was again used in 2001 as an item for the Connoisseur line. VALUE: Dark Blue: $500+; Light Blue with Cut Ruffle: $1,000+. *Courtesy of Claire and Alan Kauffung.*

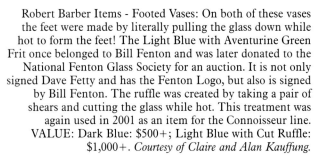

Robert Barber Items - Swirled 6.5" Vase.
VALUE: $200+. *Courtesy of Claire and Alan Kauffung.*

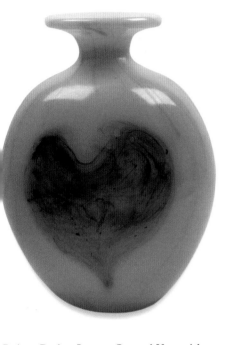

Robert Barber Items - Custard Vase with
Heart: The frit in this 9" Custard Vase was
laid out in a heart, rolled out in that shape,
and then formed into the vase. VALUE:
Custard with Heart Vase: $700+. *Courtesy of
Claire and Alan Kauffung.*

Robert Barber Items - Yellow Black 7.5" Vase/Orange-Black-
White Pulled Feather 8" Vase: VALUE: Yellow/Black 7.5"
Vase: $500+; Orange/Black/White Pulled Feather 8" Vase:
$750+. *Courtesy of Claire and Alan Kauffung.*

Robert Barber Items - Orange/Black Vases: Both vases
were made as Prototypes for the later Bittersweet Vase
that was in the regular line. VALUE: 6.75" Vase/8.5"
Vase: $750 each. *Courtesy of Claire and Alan Kauffung.*

Robert Barber Items - Orange Bowl/Ruby with Crest Bowl: What happens when a Fenton Egg is squashed? You see the results here in the Orange Bowl on the left. This item was originally made as an Egg and then squashed into a bowl while still hot. We call it a bowl here and not an ashtray, as Claire has emphatically stated that there will not be ashes in this bowl! The Ruby Bowl on the right is very unusual for a Barber item. VALUE: Orange Bowl: $500+; Ruby Bowl: $175+. *Courtesy of Claire and Alan Kauffung.*

Robert Barber Items - 3.5" Blue Feather Paperweight/4" Round Vase/6" Gray with Blue Vase: The Blue Feather Vase was made by taking a Barber Egg and using an ice pick to pull the black glass into a swirl design. The 4" Round Vase is an item that was made by Dave Fetty, who worked with Barber in this production. The Gray 6" has the familiar hanging hearts, this time in Turquoise. VALUE: Blue Feather Paperweight: $300+; 4" Round Vase: $250+; 6" Grey with Blue Vase: $250+. *Courtesy of Claire and Alan Kauffung.*

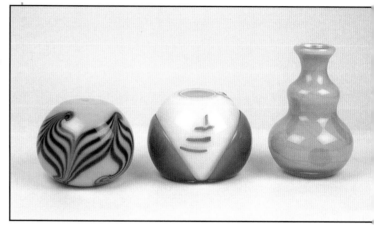

Robert Barber Items - Goblets: Unique items with the Fenton Museum Number imprinted on the bottom. Sold in the mid-1990s in the "Special Room" for FAGCA Members during the Fenton Convention. VALUE: $250+ each. *Courtesy of Claire and Alan Kauffung.*

Robert Barber Items -Turquoise/ Yellow Vase. VALUE: UND. *Courtesy of Eileen and Dale Robinson.*

Robert Barber Items - Rosalene Satin – Freehand Vase. VALUE: UND. *Courtesy of Carolyn and Dick Grable.*

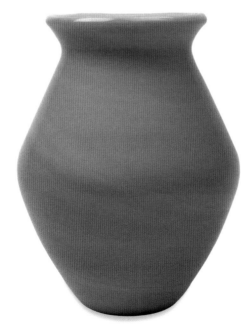

Robert Barber Hanging Hearts Items & Off Hand Items

After the trial run of the off hand items, it was decided by Fenton that the Hanging Hearts line and the Robert Barber Collection would be issued and sold in Fenton's regular line. Although every Robert Barber Collection item was individual and beautiful, the Collection did not meet with great success because of the high price involved in making it. The Barber Collection was quickly discontinued, resulting in Robert Barber leaving the company and going on to Pilgrim Glass Company. The off hand items that were in the Robert Barber Collection, marketed by Fenton, have been pictured earlier in the *Fenton Glass Compendium 1970-1985*. The items pictured below were sample items that never made it into the regular line. While any of the Hanging Heart and Robert Barber Collection items are hard to find to very scarce, these items are even more so.

Robert Barber items - Hanging Hearts - 5" Rose Bowl in Crystal Iridized: Besides the many items that were produced in freehand in 1976, the Robert Barber crew also produced many items for the Hanging Heart line, a line that was a regular production line for Fenton. The regular production items were made in Turquoise Hanging Hearts and Custard Hanging Hearts; however, they appear as Sample items in various colors. As opposed to the freehand items, which were definitely one-of-a-kinds, these items were made by having Dave Fetty and Delmar Stowasser apply the hearts (or use the pick to make the pulled feather items) and then passed them on to someone else. That individual would either blow or press them in a regular production mould or a mould that was to be used in the Barber's limited edition series. VALUE: UND. *Courtesy of Betty and Ike Hardman.*

Robert Barber Items - Hanging Hearts - Barber Bottle in Crystal Iridized: A unique color in this sample piece. Many Barber Bottle collectors would kill for this item. VALUE: UND. *Courtesy of Betty and Ike Hardman.*

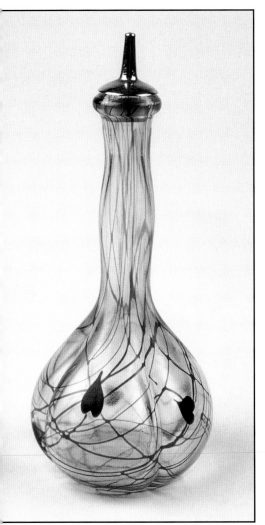

Robert Barber items - Hanging Hearts - Ruby Carnival/Custard Carnival 5" Rose Bowls: Again, items produced on regular Fenton moulds as sample items for the Hanging Hearts line. VALUE: UND. *Courtesy of Trudy and Dick Green.*

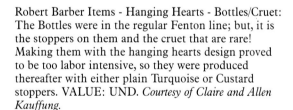

Robert Barber Items - Hanging Hearts – 6.5" Vase/Hanging Hearts Bowl: The bowl is not signed, nor has a Logo, but is suspected to be Fenton. VALUE: UND. *Courtesy of Claire and Allen Kauffung.*

Robert Barber Items - Hanging Hearts - #1921 10" Basket: While producing these sample items, Fenton used many moulds that hadn't been in used for a long while. VALUE: UND. *Courtesy of Betty and Ike Hardman.*

Robert Barber Items - Hanging Hearts - Bottles/Cruet: The Bottles were in the regular Fenton line; but, it is the stoppers on them and the cruet that are rare! Making them with the hanging hearts design proved to be too labor intensive, so they were produced thereafter with either plain Turquoise or Custard stoppers. VALUE: UND. *Courtesy of Claire and Allen Kauffung.*

Robert Barber Items - Hanging Hearts – #1921 10" Hat/ Hanging Hearts Egg: The hat is another virtually unique item, several of which have surfaced throughout the years. I originally found this item in an antique mall in northern Ohio. When I called the present owner and told her I had it, she wouldn't believe me and informed me that it didn't exist. Never say never! VALUE: UND. *Courtesy of Linda and John Flippen.*

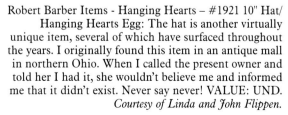

Robert Barber Items - Hanging Hearts - Handled Bottle/Custard Bottle: The Custard bottle is unique as this shape was never marketed in this color, but only in turquoise. The Handled Bottle was made off the Barber Bottle mould. VALUE: UND. *Courtesy of Claire and Allen Kauffung.*

Robert Barber Items - Hanging Hearts - #1353 Jug/Sample Tumblers: This Jug shape was never put into production. The Jug that was in regular production in the Hanging Hearts line is pictured in the *Fenton Glass Compendium 1970-85*. There are 75 of the #1353 Jugs know to exist. The Tumblers, going from left to right, are identified as follows: the last one on the right is the regular #8940 Tumbler that was sold with the Regular line pitcher; the rest were all Sample Tumblers. The barrel shape next to the pitcher is the Tumbler that matches the Pitcher. There were suppose to have been 24 of these produced. VALUE: L to R: #222 CK Tumbler: $150+; #1353 Handled Tumbler: $500; #1353 Jug: $750+; #1353 Tumbler: $150+; #1636 Ring Tumbler: $150+; Production Tumbler #8940: $65-$75. *Courtesy of Claire and Allen Kauffung.*

Robert Barber Items - Hanging Hearts - #1353 Jug with Ice Lip: Although 75 of the regular ruffled Jugs were to have been made, there are only 12 of these beauties with the ice lip, according to a former Fenton employee who was present during the production of this item. VALUE: UND. *Courtesy of Linda and John Flippen.*

Robert Barber Items - Hanging Hearts - GWTW 24" Lamp. VALUE: $2,400+. *Courtesy of Claire and Alan Kauffung.*

Robert Barber Items - Hanging Hearts - Sample Jugs/Vase. VALUE: UND. *Courtesy of Linda and John Flippen.*

Robert Barber Items - Hanging Hearts: Sample Vases. VALUE: UND. *Courtesy of Susie, Tiffany, and Ron Ballard.*

Robert Barber Items - Hanging Hearts - Square Vase. VALUE: UND. *Courtesy of Susie, Tiffany, and Ron Ballard.*

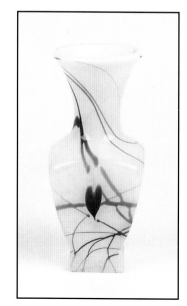

Robert Barber Items - Hanging Hearts - Cylinder Vase. VALUE: UND. *Courtesy of Linda and John Flippen.*

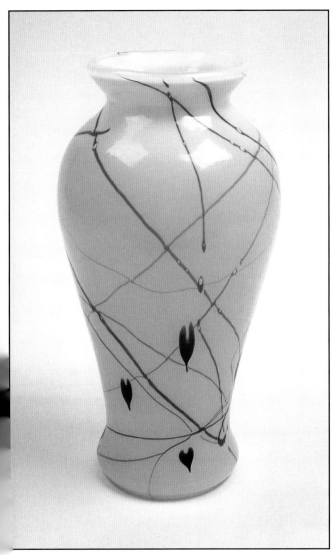

Robert Barber Items - Black & White Cascade Vase: Made in the same way as the familiar Blue and White Cascade Vase. Not in the line of the Regular Limited Edition Vases. VALUE: UND. *Courtesy of Chuck Bingham.*

Robert Barber Items - Hanging Hearts - Custard Vase. VALUE: UND. *Courtesy of Trudy and Dick Green.*

Robert Barber Items - Turquoise Hanging Heart Vase: Made in Satin, instead of the familiar Iridescent, as the regular production Limited Edition Vase. VALUE: UND. *Courtesy of Connie and Aaron Patient.*

Robert Barber Items - 11" Iridized Bittersweet Vase: The original owners of this vase were smart enough to have Bill Fenton sign it when they bought it in 1976! VALUE: $1,000+. *Courtesy of Claire and Alan Kauffung.*

Robert Barber Items - Amethyst Basket and FAGCA Vase, 1983: The Vase was made for the Fenton Art Glass Collectors of America club in 1983. The basket was produced at the same time and sold at the Whimsey auction during the FAGCA Banquet. Supposedly, two of these were produced, one was brought at the banquet by Frank Fenton, and this one was later sold to the present owner. VALUE: UND. *Courtesy of Claire and Alan Kauffung.*

Robert Barber Items - Eggs - Burmese: Possibly produced later than the regular Barber eggs. VALUE: UND. *Courtesy of John & Linda Flippen.*

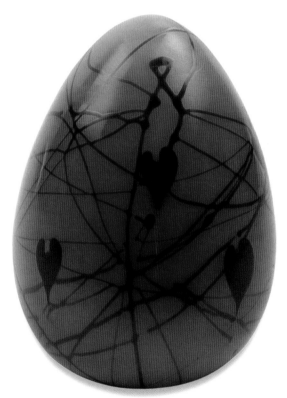

Robert Barber Items - Egg - Rosalene Hanging Hearts. VALUE: UND. *Courtesy of Randy Clark Auctions.*

Robert Barber Items? - Rosalene Hanging Hearts Vase/Black-White Vase/Purple-White Vase: It is not certain that these items are actually Barber items, but each is unique, and, to the point, even more unusual than the Barber items pictured previously. VALUE: UND. *Courtesy of Trudy and Dick Green.*

Robert Barber Items? - Wild Rose Feather Cruet/Turquoise Spanish Lace Feather Vase: Again, it's not certain if these were actually produced during the time that the Barber items were made at Fenton; but, the design of the items themselves resembles items made during this period. Notice the use of a regular production mould in the vase, maybe in an attempt to decrease the cost of producing this type of ware. VALUE: UND. *Courtesy of Trudy and Dick Green.*

Cameo Glass - Green Milk Jug: This is one of the items that, if you didn't actually pick up and see the familiar Fenton Logo, you would pass by. It seems that they experimented with Cameo Glass, possibly at the same time that Pilgrim Glass was having success with it in the late 1980s. Although no cameo treatment made it to the regular Fenton line, there were various sample items that were sold in both the Fenton Gift Shops and the Special Room during the Convention. VALUE: UND. *Courtesy of Trudy and Dick Green.*

Free Hand Items - Faverene Vases: Made some years after Robert Barber's departure.from Fenton, possibly at the time that the company was developing their Faverene treatment in the late 1980s. VALUE: UND. *Courtesy of Janice and Grody Bowerman.*

Cameo Glass - Cranberry Opaline Vase/White to Ruby Squat Vase: This shape in Cranberry Opaline, and the treatment itself, firmly dates these items to the early 1990s, when Cranberry Opaline was in the regular Fenton line. The Squat Vase is very unusual as it was made with white cased with Red Glass, and the white was entirely cut away, except for the flower design. VALUE: UND. *Courtesy of Trudy and Dick Green.*

Art Glass - Blue/White - 10" Vase, circa 1980s: Made off the same mould as the Avon Galleries Vase from 1984. Not much else is known about this beautiful piece. VALUE: UND. *Courtesy of Claire and Alan Kauffung.*

193

Burmese - Figurals - #5193 Upside Down Dolphin Paperweight/#5151 Satin Sitting Bear Cub/#5151 Shiny Bear Cub/Reclining Bear Cub/Fox/Cat: All of these items were made as samples during the transition period, going from blown items in Burmese to pressed items in Burmese. VALUE: UND. *Courtesy of Trudy and Dick Green.*

Burmese - Figurals - Glossy Sunfish/Satin Sunfish/#5171Butterfly on Stand/#5170 Butterfly off Stand/#5161 Swan/#5148 Mouse. VALUE: UND. *Courtesy of Trudy and Dick Green.*

Burmese - Alley Cat. VALUE: $200-$250. *Courtesy of Noralee and Ralph Rogers.*

Carnival - Original Formula - Butterfly. VALUE: UND. *Courtesy of Paula and Kevin Parker.*

Ruby Overlay- #5178 Large Owl: A unique item. VALUE: UND. *Courtesy of Eileen and Dale Robinson.*

Carnival - Original Formula Butterfly: This mould was originally made in Ruby Carnival for the FAGCA in the late 1970s. It's not known when this one was made, but it was probably close to the same time. The Ruby Butterfly was originally a candleholder, with holes down the back to fit the candles. This one does not have holes, making him more unique. VALUE: UND. *Courtesy of Paula and Kevin Parker.*

Carnival - Dusty Rose Iridized -Upside Down Dolphin. VALUE: UND. *Courtesy of Eileen and Dale Robinson.*

Carnival - Dusty Rose Iridized - Sunfish. VALUE: UND. *Courtesy of Eileen and Dale Robinson.*

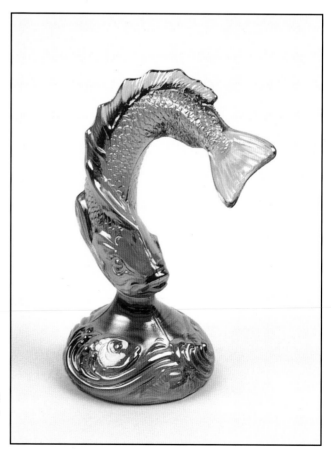

Opaque - #5171 Heavenly Blue Slag - #5171 Butterfly on Stand. VALUE: UND. *Courtesy of Paula and Kevin Parker.*

Stretch - Velva Rose - #5177 Alley Cat: Very few animals have surface in this treatment. This is probably the most desirable. VALUE: $200-$250. *Courtesy of Paula and Kevin Parker.*

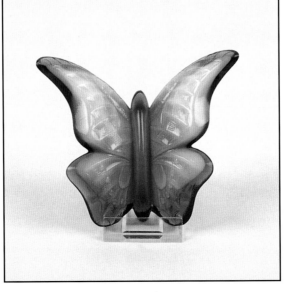

Stretch - Velva Rose - #5148 Mouse. VALUE: $80-$100. *Courtesy of Susie, Tiffany, and Ron Ballard.*

Opaque - Heavenly Blue Slag - #5170 Butterfly. VALUE: UND. *Courtesy of Paula and Kevin Parker.*

Overlay - Ruby Overlay - #5151 Bear Cub: Since he was in the regular Fenton Line for a little over a year in the 1980s, this guy seldom pops up anywhere! This is the only blown production figural that Fenton has ever made. VALUE: $100-$125. *Courtesy of Trudy and Dick Green.*

Opaque - Ruby Slag - Decorated - Bear Cub. VALUE: $125-$150: *Courtesy of Betty Hardman.*

Overlay - Ruby Overlay- #5178 Large Owl: Unique item. VALUE: UND. *Courtesy of Eileen and Dale Robinson.*

Satin - White Satin - Decorated Bridesmaid Doll: Beautiful item, given the realistic look, with delicate pastel paints and coralene. Sample item. VALUE: UND. *Courtesy of Trudy and Dick Green.*

Satin - White Satin - #5151 Corelene Decorated Bear Cub: There is not a spot on this little guy that isn't completely covered with Corelene! Made to look like a polar bear. VALUE: UND. *Courtesy of Trudy and Dick Green.*

Satin - White Decorated - #5177 Alley Cat: Seems that this Siamese Beauty decided to go slumming it as an Alley Cat! This is a very unusual and desirable item. VALUE: UND. *Courtesy of Paula and Kevin Parker.*

Satin - White Decorated - Alley Cat: Back side.

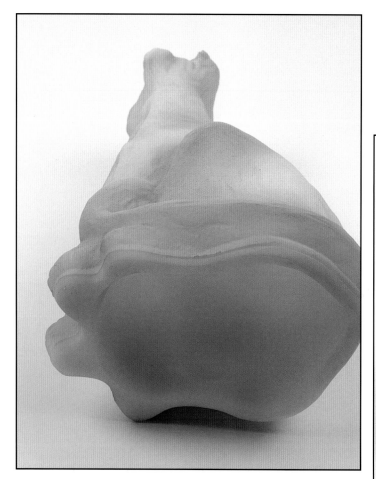

Satin - White Decorated - Alley Cat: Interior view.

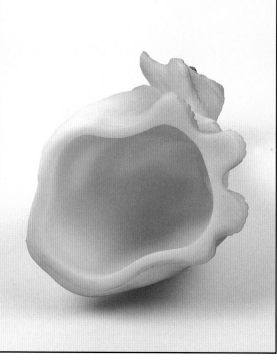

Satin - White Decorated - Alley Cat.

Satin - Various Colors - #5197 Happiness Birds: Many in different colors; decorations have appeared on this and other animals throughout the years, most of which sold in the Gift Shop. VALUE: $50-$70 each. *Courtesy of Jan Hollingsworth.*

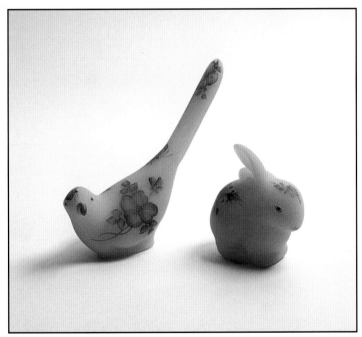

Satin - Lavender Satin - #5197 Happiness Bird/#5162 Bunny: When you see these animals in person, it makes a person wonders why Fenton did not produce a line of items in Decorated Lavender Satin. VALUE: UND. *Courtesy of Killcreek Antiques.*

Transparent - Topaz Satin - #5160 Fawn. VALUE: UND. *Courtesy of Jan Hollingsworth.*

Transparent - Colonial Orange - Butterfly on Stand.
VALUE: UND. *Courtesy of Doris Grajczyk.*

Transparent - Colonial Orange -
#5163 Small Bird. VALUE: UND.

Transparent - Colonial Orange - Star on Stand: Possibly made as a Christmas orna-
ment. This is a good example of how most of the Fenton Figurals are produced. They
are originally made on this type of a stand and then cut off, the bottom of the figural
are finished and polished, and then the stand is remelted and used again to make
other glass. VALUE: UND. *Courtesy of Eileen and Dale Robinson.*

Transparent - Ruby - Cat/Reclining Bear.
VALUE: Cat: $55-$65; Bear: $75-$85. *Courtesy
of Dick and Trudy Green.*

Transparent - Smoke - Elephant, circa 1985. VALUE: $125-$150. *Courtesy of Bev and Jon Spencer.*

Vasa Murrhina - Elephants: Due to a huge mistake created by not doing enough research on the book that the Elephants, Birds, and Mushrooms in Vasa Murrhina were pictured in earlier, I recorded too low of a price for these guys. Not only is this deep blue color treatment extremely rare, but also (to clarify) *all* the Vasa Figurals are rare and desirable. VALUE: Elephants: $150-$175; Birds: $125-$150; Mushrooms: $150-$175.

Overlay - Fruit, circa 1980s: At first look one would swear that this grouping of glass fruit is Murno, but that is not the case. The Banana, for example, is made out of Candleglow Yellow Overlay, the Apple is Cased Cranberry, and all these pieces are definitely Fenton! This grouping of Fruit was produced in the mid-1980s at the same time of the Overlay Apples shown in the *Fenton Glass Compendium 1970-85.* UND. *Courtesy of Betty and Ike Hardman.*

Carnival - Orange Carnival - #8265 Lily of the Valley Bell: Another good example of a mould that was produced in many different colors during the 1970s, appearing in an unlisted color. This seemed to have happened a lot in this time period, and one could almost expect that any mould used during the 1970s time period could pop up in a color other than what was listed in the regular Fenton catalogs and files. VALUE: UND. *Courtesy of Mala Foust.*

Opaque - Pekin Blue - #5140 Decorated Egg: An egg in this color is rare enough in itself, but to find one that is decorated is completely unique. VALUE: UND. *Courtesy of Betty and Ike Hardman.*

Opaque/Opalescent - Large/Medium Eggs - Pink Opaque/Cranberry Splatter Opalescent. VALUE: UND. *Courtesy of Trudy and Dick Green.*

Decorated Milk Glass - Santa Fairy Light. VALUE: $100-$150. *Courtesy of Carol Toumlin.*

Overlay - Ruby Overlay - Fairy Light: Although in the regular Fenton line, this Fairy Light is very uncommon. VALUE: $100-$125. *Courtesy of Trudy and Dick Green.*

Satin - White Satin - Madonna Prayer Light: Items like this, that are completely decorated to have a realistic effect, are very uncommon. VALUE: UND. *Courtesy of Eileen and Dale Robinson.*

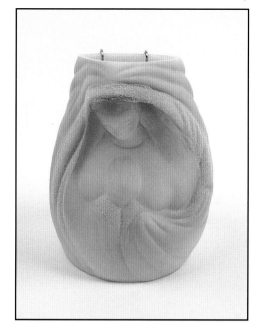

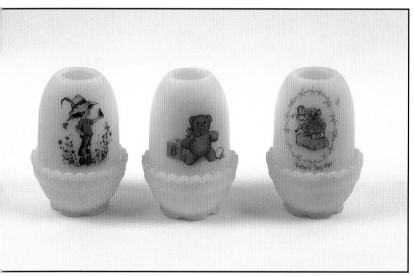

Satin - Custard Satin - Assorted Fairy Lights. VALUE: $60-$80 each. *Courtesy of Carol Toumlin.*

Satin - Custard Satin - Train Fairy Light: "THE GENERAL," circa mid-1980s: This pattern was made in several shapes, including a plate, a lamp, and a fairy light. The way this pattern came into being is quite unique. Fenton held a design contest, announcing that they would retain the winning design for their own use, and the losing artist could keep the pieces that they produced. Each artist were given a lamp shade to make the design on. Carol Shaffer, the designer of "The General," wanted to give a lamp with a train design on it to her father, who was a train enthusiast. Figuring that she would lose the contest and be given the shade, she entered this design. Although it did not win the design contest, Fenton special ordered this pattern for sale in limited quantities in the Gift Shop, in the above mentioned items. This one fairy light is quite unique, as the original owner asked Carol Shaffer to paint the fish (a Red Salomon) on it after she purchased the piece for her grandson. VALUE: UND. *Courtesy of Jan Hollinsworth.*

Satin - Custard Satin - Assorted Fairy Lights. VALUE: $60-$80 each. *Courtesy of Carol Toumlin.*

Opaque - Decorated Milk Glass - Logo with Roses. VALUE: UND. *Courtesy of Trudy and Dick Green.*

Crest - Decorated Apple Blossom: This lamp, along with the decorated Honey Amber Overlay pictured later, was produced in the mid-to-late 1960s, right after Fenton started its own lamp department and production of Lamps for themselves. This is the only piece of Apple Blossom to have been produced in the regular Fenton line since the issue of the pattern in 1961. VALUE: $500-$600. *Courtesy of Eileen and Dale Robinson.*

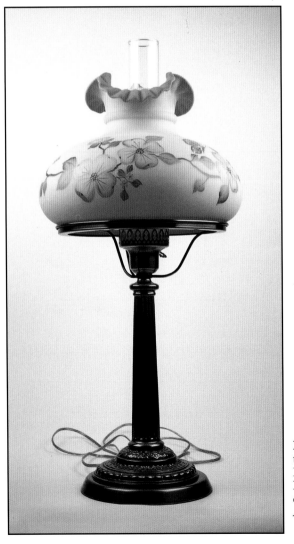

Crest - Blue Ridge: This lamp was produced at the same time as the 80th Anniversary Blue Ridge Series was issued in 1985. No record of this lamp exists to assert that it was ever in the regular line. It was probably made as a sample item. VALUE: UND. *Courtesy of Chuck Bingham.*

Burmese - Pink Dogwood: Another example of the talents of the many artist and decorators at Fenton. This lamp was never in the Pink Dogwood line, but is an added asset to any collection. VALUE: UND. *Courtesy of Paula and Kevin Parker.*

Opalescent - Coin Dot - Honeysuckle: Made in the 1960s, much later than the regular issue of Honeysuckle Coindot. Lamps and Lamp founts in this color were made throughout the 1950s and into the early 1970s. VALUE: $400-$500. *Courtesy of Janice and Gordy Bowerman.*

Opalescent - Poppy GWTW - Topaz Opalescent: An absolutely breathtaking item, made in the late 1970s or early 1980s, when Topaz Opalescent came back into the Fenton line. VALUE: $600-$700. *Courtesy of Susie, Tiffany, and Ron Ballard.*

Overlay - Opaque Blue Satin Overlay - Poppy GWTW Lamp: Another fabulous lamp from the 1970s. This was also a treatment which Fenton had not used for several years, and had brought back to sample this item. VALUE: UND. *Courtesy of Adonna and Elmer Punslar.*

Overlay - Decorated Honey Amber: Made at the same time as the Apple Blossom Lamp pictured previously. Both of these lamps were produced circa 1969, as the decorating department was not in existence until shortly before that time period. VALUE: $300-$400. *Courtesy of Eileen and Dale Robinson.*

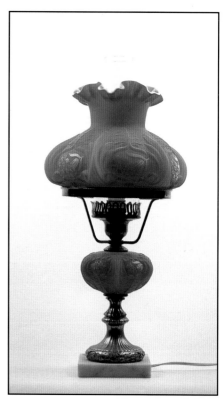

Overlay - Opaque Blue Satin Overlay - HP Student Lamp. VALUE: UND. *Courtesy Eileen and Dale Robinson.*

Overlay - Shelly Green Overlay - Poppy Table Lamp: Unusual size globe, it is smaller than the regular GWTW globe. It is not certain whether this is the correct base for this lamp. VALUE: $200-$250. *Courtesy of Eileen and Dale Robinson.*

Overlay - Vasa Murrhina - Banquet Lamp: These were in Fenton's catalog in Burmese, Opaque Blue Overlay, Milk Glass, and Ruby Overlay in the Rose Pattern; however, no record exists of this beauty. VALUE: UND. *Courtesy of Susie, Tiffany, and Ron Ballard.*

Overlay - Vasa Murrhina - "Ginger Jar" Table Lamp: Made from the Table Lamp that Fenton produced in the mid-1960s to go along with the regular Vasa Murrhina line. This lamp, which had lost its original fittings and cloth shade, was reworked and fashioned into a Ginger Jar type lamp. It just shows, with a little imagination and work, what can be accomplished with the lamp parts! VALUE: UND. *Courtesy of Susie, Tiffany, and Ron Ballard.*

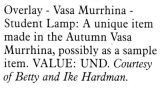

Overlay - Vasa Murrhina - Student Lamp: A unique item made in the Autumn Vasa Murrhina, possibly as a sample item. VALUE: UND. *Courtesy of Betty and Ike Hardman.*

Satin - Rose Satin - Poppy Lamp: I know that this is not a correct Fenton lamp, although the glass part is definitely Fenton. But this gives you an idea of what you can do with the bottom when you break the globe of a lamp. In this case, the bottom was taken apart and rewired, making it a one piece lamp. VALUE: UND. *Courtesy of Susie, Ron, and Tiffany Ballard.*

Satin - Decorated Satin - Chickadee Lamp: This lamp is made up very much the same way as the previous lamp; however, in this case it looks as if this might actually be the globe. VALUE: UND. *Courtesy of Sharon and Alan Fenner.*

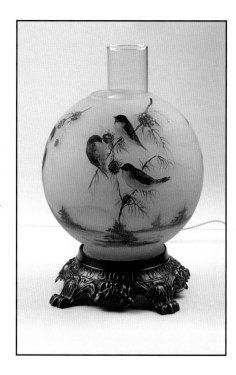

Overlay - Colonial Orange - Student Lamp. VALUE: $250-$300.

Bibliography

Books

Fenton Art Glass Collectors of America. *Caught in the Butter Fly Net.* Williamstown, West Virginia: Fenton Art Glass Club of America, Inc., 1991.

_____. *Fenton Catalog Pages.* Reprint. Williamstown, West Virginia: Fenton Art Glass Of America, Inc., 1986.

Florence, Gene. *Collectible Glassware from the 40's 50's 60's.* Paducah, Kentucky: Schroeder, 1st/2nd/3rd Editions 1992, 1994, 1996.

Griffith, Shirley. *Pictorial Review of Fenton's White Hobnail Milk Glass.* N.p., 1994.

Heacock, William. *Fenton Glass: The 2nd Twenty Five Years.* Marietta, Ohio: O-Val Advertising Corp., 1980.

_____. *Fenton Glass: The 3rd Twenty Five Years.* Marietta, Ohio: O-Val Advertising Corp., 1989.

_____. *Victorian Colored Pattern Glass, Book II: Opalescent Glass, A to Z.* Marietta, Ohio: Antique Publications, 1975.

_____. *Victorian Colored Pattern Glass, Book III: Syrups, Sugar Shakers, A to Z.* Marietta, Ohio: Antique Publications, 1976.

Heacock, William and William Gamble. *Victorian Colored Pattern Glass Book IX: Cranberry Opalescent Glass, A to Z.* Marietta, Ohio: Antique Publications, 1987.

Lafferty, James, Sr. *The Forties Revisited.* James Lafferty, Sr., 1968.

Lecher, Mildred and Ralph. *The World of Salt Shakers.* Paducah, Kentucky: Schroeder, 1992.

Measell, James (ed). *Fenton Glass: The 80's Decade.* Marietta, Ohio: Antique Publications, 1996.

_____. *Fenton Glass: The 90's Decade.* Marietta, Ohio: Antique Publications, 2000.

Walk, John. *Fenton Glass Compendium, 1940-70.* Atglen, Pennsylvania: Schiffer Publishing, 1991.

_____. *Fenton Glass Compendium, 1970-85.* Atglen, Pennsylvania: Schiffer Publishing, 1991.

Walk, John and Joseph Gates. *The Big Book of Fenton Glass, 1940-70.* 1st and 2nd Editions. Atglen, Pennsylvania: Schiffer Publishing, 1998.

Whitmyer, Margaret and Kenn. *Bedroom and Bathroom Glassware of the Depression Years.* Paducah, Kentucky: Schroeder, 1990.

_____. *Fenton Art Glass Patterns: 1939-80.* Paducah, Kentucky, Schroeder, n.d.

Periodicals

Depression Glass Daze (1980-1997).
Glass Collector's Digest (1986-1997).
Glass Review (1978-1987).